Christopher J. H. Wright

Knowing
God the Father

Through the
Old Testament

IVP Academic
An imprint of InterVarsity Press
Downers Grove, Illinois

InterVarsity Press
P.O. Box 1400, Downers Grove, IL 60515-1426
Internet: www.ivpress.com
E-mail: email@ivpress.com

InterVarsity Press® is the book-publishing division of InterVarsity Christian Fellowship/USA®, a student movement
active on campus at hundreds of universities, colleges and schools of nursing in the United States of America, and a
member movement of the International Fellowship of Evangelical Students. For information about local and regional
activities, write Public Relations Dept., InterVarsity Christian Fellowship/USA, 6400 Schroeder Rd., P.O. Box 7895,
Madison, WI 53707-7895, or visit the IVCF website at <www.intervarsity.org>.

Cover design: Cindy Kiple

Cover image: Alinari/Art Resource, NY

ISBN 978-0-8308-2592-9

Printed in the United States of America

Library of Congress Cataloging-in-Publication Data

Wright, Christopher J. H., 1947-
  Knowing God the Father through the Old Testament / Christopher J.H.
Wright.
      p. cm.
  Includes bibliographical references and index.
  ISBN-13: 978-0-8308-2592-9 (pbk.: alk. paper)
  1. God—Fatherhood—Biblical teaching. 2. Bible. O.T.—Criticism,
interpretation, etc. I. Title.
  BS1192.6.W75 2007
  231′.1—dc22
                                                                            2007026756

P   18   17   16   15   14   13   12   11   10   9   8   7   6   5   4   3   2   1
Y   22   21   20   19   18   17   16   15   14   13   12   11   10   09   08   07

To

John Stott

Contents

Preface

Years ago, teaching the Old Testament at the Union Biblical Seminary in Pune, India, I used to set as a research topic, "The Knowledge of God in the Book of Hosea"—or in some other specified part of the Old Testament. It was always fascinating to observe the sense of excitement that students had as they returned from a voyage of considerable discovery and reported what they had found. I told myself that some day I would speak or write on the same subject in greater depth myself.

So when I was asked to give the Bible expositions at the annual conference of the European Christian Mission in April 2002, I chose "Knowing God" as my theme. So it was that five expositions which underlie several of the chapters of this book were first delivered by the beautiful Lake Bled in Slovenia. I am grateful to ECM and the conference organizers for that invitation.

It had long seemed to me that the theme of knowing God had tended to be handled either in a systematic or thematic way (as in the brilliant classic with that title by J. I. Packer), or in a purely personal and devotional way, largely devoid of Old Testament content. And yet it is clear (or I hope it will be by the end of this book) that knowing God is a theme that could claim to be one of the more major concerns of the Bible, and particularly of the Old Testament.

Having written *Knowing Jesus Through the Old Testament* some years ago, and then having followed it more recently with *Knowing the Holy Spirit Through the Old Testament*, it seemed natural to complete the trilogy with this volume, incorporating the Old Testament's teaching about God as Father within the wider theme of knowing God as such. At least one can be confident that no further additions to such a series will be called for.

I owe my thanks to all who have helped and encouraged me along the way, including as always my family. I am especially grateful to the Langham Partnership International for insisting in my contract that I take some time for writing each year—which is why I am delighted to assign all royalties to Langham Literature. With great affection and gratitude I dedicate the book to Rev. Dr. John Stott, at whose cottage in Wales (the Hookses) most of it was written, and whose friendship, encouragement and prayers in relation to all my ministry are as precious beyond words as he himself is.

Chris Wright
November 2006

Introduction

When you pray, say, "Our Father in heaven . . ."

With these words Jesus introduced his disciples to a whole new dimension of prayer. Not that they did not already know how to pray—even though we might think that from their question, "Lord, teach us to pray" (Lk 11:1). The faith of Israel was a praying faith, and the disciples of Jesus belonged to a people for whom the prayers and praises of the Psalms were woven into the fabric of their daily lives as much as their everyday food (which never passed their lips without prayer). The point of their question seems to have been, "Lord, teach us to pray *like you do*." For clearly the prayer life of Jesus went beyond anything they knew themselves, or even anything they had observed among the professional prayer experts (about whom Jesus had some less-than-flattering things to say).

One major dimension of that prayer life of Jesus (something that probably surprised, puzzled and perhaps shocked them), was the familiarity with which Jesus addressed God as Father. They could see that Jesus had a unique, intimate relation with God as *his* Father, whom he addressed in the family language of "Abba." But could such a way of relating and speaking to God in prayer be available also to his followers? With his classic template of prayer, Jesus says that it is not only possible, but it is to be normal and standard. And so ever since then followers of Jesus have entered effortlessly (though sometimes routinely and without thought) into the limitless relational richness of calling God "Father."

Calling God "Father" in prayer is second nature to *Christian* believers, but it seems that it was surprising to Jesus' first disciples. Why was that? The simple reason is that it was not the common way of addressing God within the worshiping life of Israel. Now this is not because the ancient Israelites did not know of God as Father—both the concept and the terminology are most definitely there in the Scriptures of Israel that we call the Old Testament, and we shall explore them further below. But "Father" is not the common or normal form of address to God in the Old Testament. It is not used, for example, in the book of Israelite hymns and prayers[1]—the Book of Psalms, even though that book abounds in other ways of speaking about God and to God.

So the question must arise, then, in the mind of anybody contemplating the title of this book: how can so many pages be filled with a theme that is so apparently slender in the Old Testament itself? Is it not somewhat forced or anachronistic to talk about "knowing God the Father *through the Old Testament*"? Surely this is something that we can really only discuss, as Christians, in the light of the New Testament, and that fuller revelation of God through his Son Jesus Christ. Indeed, it is in knowing Jesus as the *Son of God* that we know more clearly about the *Father* (as Jesus himself told his disciples). And then from that point we move toward the more developed understanding of the trinitarian nature of God as Father, Son and Holy Spirit.

Well, of course all this is true, to a point. But we are still left with

---

[1]Except once as a form of address by the Davidic king (Ps 89:26), and in a few metaphorical verses that we shall look at in chapter 1.

the biblical fact that Old Testament Israel did know a thing or two about the living God, and they *did* on occasions call their God Father—even if other titles and forms of address are much more common. And they certainly used the role, expectations and responsibilities of human fathers as a way of speaking about certain aspects of God. That is to say, there are fatherly portraits and metaphors for God, even when he is not directly called Father.

So another way of putting our question would be this: Is the God of the Old Testament revelation—the God whom Israel knew as Yahweh (though by the time of Jesus already, probably, they had ceased to pronounce this name, and substituted for it either *Adonai*—"the Lord," or *Ha Shem*—"the Name")[2]—is that God the same as the God we call Father? In other words, can we equate Yahweh of Old Testament faith and affirmation with God the Father in our trinitarian understanding of God? I believe we can say yes, with some careful qualifications, for the following reasons.

THE UNITY OF THE TRINITY

Christians do not believe in three Gods. It is of the very essence of trinitarian confession that God is One. We believe that truth just as strongly as Israelite believers did when they recited the Shema, "Hear, O Israel: the LORD our God, the LORD is one" (Deut 6:4). So on the assumption that the God revealed in the Old Testament is the one true living God whom we also now know in the fullness of his final revelation through his incarnation in Jesus of Nazareth and the outpouring of his Holy Spirit at Pentecost, we must also affirm that all

---

[2]The earliest Greek translations of the Hebrew Scriptures (made well over a hundred years before Christ), followed this practice, and rendered the divine name YHWH as *ho kyrios*—"the Lord." In the same tradition, English translations use the capitalized form "the LORD" to render the personal name of God in the Old Testament. It is worth remembering, when we read this term—that it represents a personal name, not just a title.

three persons of the Godhead (as we now call them), are "contained" within the singular, integrated personal identity of the God who chose to be known as Yahweh in the Old Testament.

The great affirmation of Deuteronomy 4:35 and 39 affirms not only the uniqueness but also the universality and completeness of Yahweh as God.

> The LORD is God in heaven above and on the earth below. There is no other. (Deut 4:39)

This means not only that Yahweh is the *only* God there is, but Yahweh is also *all* the God there is, or to put it another way, Yahweh is all there is to God. There is no higher deity above or behind him, or a better one to come after him. Yahweh is not just the penultimate name for some more ultimate divine reality. Deity as such, in every sense that can be affirmed within and beyond the universe—deity is defined by Yahweh. God *is* as he is revealed to be in the person of *this* God, and no other. This being so, then all that we would now strive to express about God through our doctrine of the Trinity is already encapsulated in the transcendent, unique, and universal God Yahweh. The Israelites may not have known all that just yet, but that does not mean it was not the objective reality and truth about God.[3]

This means that it is usually rather pointless (in my view), to ask about any Old Testament verse that speaks about Yahweh, which person of the Trinity it is referring to. There are some places where the Spirit of Yahweh is clearly indicated (as I surveyed in *Knowing the Holy Spirit Through the Old Testament),* and there are certainly messi-

---

[3] That is to say, if you like this kind of language and you can forget it if you don't, that we can make a distinction between the epistemological dimension (what Israel at any given point in their history *knew* about God, through his action and revelation to that point), and the onto-logical dimension (all that God actually *is,* and always has been, in his own divine reality).

anic texts (in intention, or in later canonical reading) in which we can identify the pre-incarnate second person of the Trinity whom we now know through Jesus of Nazareth. Furthermore, it is also clear that in the New Testament, the most remarkable thing that happened in the faith of the earliest followers of Jesus is that they came to identify *him, Jesus,* with Yahweh, in calling him Lord, and in many other ways.[4] So, yes, it is certainly true from a whole-Bible perspective, that the God Yahweh of the Old Testament "embodies" (if that is not too human a word), the Son and the Holy Spirit. But on the whole it is probably more appropriate in most cases that when we read about Yahweh, we should have God the Father in mind.

THE PRIMARY FUNCTIONS OF YAHWEH

When Old Testament Israelites made their great affirmation about the transcendent uniqueness of Yahweh, they frequently associated it with major roles or functions that were attributed to him. The most outstanding was that Yahweh alone is the Creator of everything else that exists apart from himself (e.g., Jer 10:11-12). A second was that Yahweh alone is king. He is supreme ruler, not only over Israel, but over all nations, and the whole of creation (e.g., Deut 10:14, 17). And a third was that Yahweh is the ultimate judge of all human behavior—from the smallest individual thought and action to the macrocosm of international relations in the ebb and flow of history (e.g., Ps 33:13-15). Creator, king and judge: in all these spheres the sovereign universality of Yahweh was affirmed again and again. And these are typically the roles that are commonly associated with the person of God the Father. "I believe in God the Father Almighty, Creator of

---

[4] See Christopher J. H. Wright, *The Mission of God: Unlocking the Bible's Grand Narrative* (Downers Grove, Ill.: InterVarsity Press, 2006), chap. 4, "The Living God Makes Himself Known in Jesus Christ."

heaven and earth" we recite, in the Apostles' Creed, for example.

Now of course, we have to agree that one of the major ways in which the New Testament affirms the identity of *Jesus* with Yahweh (and thereby implying his deity), is through attributing all of these primary divine roles to the Lord Jesus Christ as well—and adding another, the role of Savior (which was another major defining characteristic of Yahweh). In the New Testament, *Jesus* is portrayed as Creator, king, Savior and judge.[5] All this goes to demonstrate the unity of the Godhead in all the ways in which God acts. Paul combines both the Father and Jesus in his remarkable expansion of the Shema in 1 Corinthians:

> There is but one God, the Father, from whom all things came and for whom we live; and there is but one Lord, Jesus Christ, through whom all things came and through whom we live. (1 Cor 8:6)

Nevertheless, the more common way of differentiating at a conceptual level between the persons of God is to associate the roles of creating, sustaining, ordering, ruling and judging the earth and all its inhabitants with God the Father. For this reason, again, it is natural to associate the name and character of Yahweh in the Old Testament primarily (though not, as we have said, exclusively) with the Father.

THE GOD TO WHOM JESUS PRAYED

Jesus was fully human. He grew up in a devout and believing Jewish home, and was without doubt a worshiping, praying child, young man and adult. The daily habit of prayer that we read of in the Gospels must have been ingrained in him from childhood. So when Jesus

---

[5]Ibid.

worshiped and prayed, in his home or in the synagogue in Nazareth, to whom was his worship directed? Who was the God whose name he read in all the Scriptures he recited and all the songs he sang? To whom did Jesus pray at the knees of Mary and then through all his life? The answer is, of course, to the LORD, Yahweh (though he would have said *Adonai*). Jesus would have recited the Shema daily with his fellow Jews, and he knew the "LORD our God" of that text to be the God of his people, his human parents and himself. So Jesus' whole perception of God was entirely shaped by the Scriptures we call the Old Testament. When Jesus thought of God, spoke of God, reflected on the words and will of God, set out to obey God—it was *this* God, Yahweh God, that was in his mind. "God" for Jesus was the named, biographied, character-rich, self-revealed God Yahweh, the Holy One of Israel. When Jesus and his disciples talked together of God, this is the name they would have used (or would have known but piously avoided pronouncing). When Jesus read Isaiah 61 in the synagogue in Nazareth, he claimed that the Spirit of the LORD was upon him "to-day"—the Spirit of Yahweh, God of the Old Testament prophets.

But of course, Jesus also knew this God of his Scriptures in the depth of his self-consciousness as *Abba,* as his own intimate personal Father. Luke tells us that this awareness was developing even in his childhood, and it was sealed at his baptism, when he heard the voice of his Father, accompanied by the Holy Spirit, confirming his identity as God's beloved Son. So in the consciousness of Jesus the *scriptural* identity of God as Yahweh and his *personal* intimacy with God as his Father must have blended together. The God he knew from his Bible as Yahweh was the God he knew in prayer as his Father. When Jesus took the Psalms on his lips on the cross, the God he was calling out to in the agony of abandonment was the God addressed in Psalm 22:1 as Elohim, but throughout the psalm as Yahweh. The psalmist was calling out to Yahweh. Jesus uses his words to call out to his Father.

Now since all our understanding of God as Father must start out from knowing Jesus, it makes sense for us also to think of Yahweh, the God of Old Testament Israel and the God of the one true faithful Israelite Jesus, as God the Father, for that is who Yahweh primarily was in the consciousness of Jesus himself.

So then, an important foundational assumption for the rest of this book is just this, that knowing God as Father in the Old Testament is really a dimension of simply *knowing God*—that is, of knowing Yahweh as God. And that perception opens up for us a horizon of great breadth and vistas of rich biblical content. *Knowing God,* or the knowledge of God, is one of the truly immense themes of the Old Testament. It is challenging, frightening and encouraging. It can be intimate and devotional, but it is also deeply practical and ethical. It applies to individuals and to nations. It looks to the past and fills the intentions of God for the future. This will be a voyage of exciting and challenging biblical discovery.

However, as I said, the Israelites did sometimes actually speak of God as Father, even though we have to recognize that it was not a prominent or common dimension of their language of worship (not anything like the extent of its prominence in the New Testament). So we shall certainly also explore this theme of the fatherhood of God in the faith of Israel, and this too should lead us in a journey around some texts and concepts that are rather off the usual tourist routes of the Old Testament. So then, we shall weave our way in the chapters that follow through a twin theme. Sometimes the main emphasis will be on "knowing God" as we look at texts where that theme is in the foreground. Sometimes the main emphasis will be on God as Father in texts where that is a dominant metaphor. Our hope is that the combination and interaction of these themes and texts will enrich and deepen our personal understanding of, and relationship with, the biblical God.

One final observation before we set forth. Our title is obviously framed from the common trinitarian formulation—"God the Father." This in itself, as we have seen, is not a term that the Old Testament uses in quite that form. And it would be unfortunate if our reflections in the course of this book on the fatherhood of God were misinterpreted to imply some kind of harsh patriarchal authoritarianism. Certainly the metaphor of human fatherhood is used as a way of speaking about certain key characteristics of God. But so is the metaphor of motherhood. In fact, the language of parenthood, in both genders, is explicitly used in relation to God as early as Deuteronomy 32:18. Likewise, should human parenthood fail (whether father or mother), the psalmist looks to God to fulfill their dual role in caring for him (Ps 27:10). Another psalmist compares his attentive dependence on God to a maid looking to her mistress. And God himself draws remarkable self-comparisons to a pregnant mother in labor (Is 42:14) and a nursing mother breastfeeding her child (Is 49:15). Apart from these explicitly motherly metaphors for God in the Old Testament, we shall observe (especially in chapter one), that the language of fatherhood, while it certainly includes appropriate exercise and expectations of authority, is commonly also associated with love, care, compassion, provision, protection and sustenance.

1

Knowing God as a Father in Action

When I arrived in my first parish as a newly ordained curate (assistant pastor), I was responsible for coordinating the team of youth leaders. One of the other curates, who had done this job for the previous two years, was commending a young married couple who were part of the team. "They are pure gold," he said to me. I had not even met them yet, but he knew them very well, and that was the metaphor he chose to explain to me their high quality and great value. The better we know someone, the more we find metaphors that sum up what they are like and what they mean to us. "She's a pillar of the community." "He's the life and soul of the party." "She's like a rock for her whole family." "He's a walking volcano." "She's an oasis of common sense." "He's a loose cannon." "She's a bit of a butterfly."

The Bible is rich in metaphors for God, and for the same reason. We are invited to know God as deeply and intimately as is humanly possible. And the more we know God, the more we will find ways of expressing who he is and what he means to us. Knowing God is one of the richest themes in the Old Testament. It is something that takes many different shapes, and happens in many different contexts. Not surprisingly, then, the Old Testament is rich in metaphors that people of faith used to describe the God they had come to know in all these ways.

We are familiar with the commonest of these, since they dominate the landscape of Old Testament faith, worship and theology. Yahweh is king, judge and redeemer. Those are human images. There are other less common human analogies, like Yahweh as shepherd, as teacher, as soldier, as farmer. And of course there are many non-human metaphors also: Yahweh is a rock, a shelter, a shield, a hiding place, a lion, fire, a spring of water, etc.

Surprisingly, the metaphor of God as Father is not as common as we might have expected. As we shall see in a moment, the Israelites certainly did not overlook the rich store of metaphorical meaning in thinking of Yahweh their God in relation to the common human experience of fatherhood. But they were reticent with the concept of Yahweh as Father at one level (in worship), while quite free with it at another (in personal names).

Only rather rarely do Old Testament texts speak about, or speak to, Yahweh as Father in contexts of worship or devotion. In the book of Psalms, for example, God is only once referred to as "my Father" (by the king, in Psalm 89:26, and never directly by any psalmist), and God is compared to a human father only three times (see below). The most likely reason for this is that Israel chose to reject the pagan and mythological notions of divine parenthood that were common in surrounding religions. In the polytheistic environment, gods and goddesses engaged in sexual congress and gave birth to all kinds of phenomena, including some nations. The monotheistic faith of Israel rejected such a view of the relationship between Yahweh and Israel. Israel had not been literally conceived and birthed by Yahweh, or by any female goddess with whom Yahweh had consorted to produce offspring. So while they certainly made use of familial metaphors (husband-wife, conception and birth, parent-child) to portray the relationship, they did not elevate them into primary forms of address to God or of discourse about God. And when they did use them, they were very careful to rule out the pagan mythical conceptions.

So, for example, Jeremiah parodies the sexual fertility cult of the Canaanites, which had badly infected Israel in his day. They used a standing stone to symbolize the phallic sacred male, and a tree or a wooden pole to symbolize the sacred female. Jeremiah mocks the worship of this sexual pairing that was credited with some kind of divine parenthood by the worshiper—reversing the polarity.

> They say to wood, "You are my father,"
> and to stone, "You gave me birth." (Jer 2:27)

If this was the way people used "my father" in worship, it's no wonder the orthodox Old Testament faith tended to avoid it.

And yet, while somewhat reticent to address God as Father in the context of worship, Israel was quite free in using the idea of Yahweh as Father in another way—and that is in the area of personal names. The word *theophoric* is used to describe human names that include part or all of the name of a god. My own name, for example, Christopher (which is Greek, meaning, "Christ-bearer") is theophoric. So are Theodore, or Dorothy (gift of God), and Timothy (honored by God). Most cultures are rich in theophoric names. The names of the Babylonian gods, Bel and Nebo, for example, are found in Belshazzar and Nebuchadnezzar. In India, names compounded from Ram and Krishna are very common. Abdulla (servant of Allah) is common in Arabic speaking nations. And so on.

El is one of the commonest names for God (the high God across the whole ancient Near East). And Yahweh was often shortened to *Yah*, or *Yeho*, or *Yo*. Thus, the wide range of Israelite names that begin or end with El (Eliezer, Elimelech, Nathaniel, etc.); or that begin with Jeho-, or Jo- (Jehoshaphat, Joshua, Jonathan); or end in -iah, or -ijah

(Obadiah, Elijah, Azariah, Adonijah)—are all theophoric. They are little phrases, or affirmations about God or Yahweh, built into a personal name.

Now in Hebrew, the word for father is *ab*. "My father" is *abi*. So when *ab* or *abi* is put together with *el* or one of the abbreviations of Yahweh, then the name becomes a statement about God as Father, or as "my Father." So, we have the following possibilities—all attested in the names of the Old Testament.

Abiel	God is my father (1 Sam 9:1)
Eliab	My God is father (1 Sam 16:6)
Joab	Yahweh is father (2 Sam 8:16)
Abijah	Yahweh is my father (this can be a man or woman's name—see 2 Chron 29:1)
Abimelech	My father is king (where "king" probably refers to God, Judg 9:1)

The common occurrence of these names shows that the idea of God, or Yahweh, as father was well known and accepted. After all, a person called Abijah walking around the place was making a theological statement—"Yahweh is my father"—every time he gave his name, or was greeted by others. Parents who decided to call their son "Joab," "Yahweh is Father," had some metaphoric understanding of his and their relationship to Yahweh as father. So even if the term was not on the lips of Israelites in regular worship, it was on their lips in everyday speech as they used their own common names.

What message, then, did the metaphor contain? In this chapter we shall look at some general aspects of what it meant to call God Father, or to compare him with human fathers. In the next chapter we shall look more particularly at how the relationship between God and Israel as a nation (which was much more commonly described as a covenant, of course), could be seen in father-son terms, and what that implied.

So let us open up some rather warm-hearted Old Testament texts in which we will discover that God can be portrayed as

- the Father who carries his children, in whom we can trust
- the Father who disciplines his children, to whom we should submit
- the Father who pities his children, to whom we should be grateful
- the Father who adopts the homeless or fatherless, in whom we find security

GOD—THE FATHER WHO CARRIES

> The LORD your God, who is going before you, will fight for you, as he did for you in Egypt, before your very eyes, and in the desert. There you saw how *the LORD your God carried you, as a father carries his son*, all the way you went until you reached this place. (Deut 1:30-31, italics added)

We have all seen a father pick up and carry a child in his arms, on his back or shoulders. Usually it is because the child is tired, or the terrain is difficult or dangerous—and sometimes it is because the child is being fractious and disobedient. There's something of all these in the picture Moses paints here.

Moses' memoirs of Israel's journeying since leaving Egypt fill Deuteronomy 1—3. By the start of Deuteronomy, Israel had reached the plains of Moab, just across the Jordan from the Promised Land. But it had been a long and convoluted journey. In fact, as Deuteronomy 1:2-3 laconically points out, a journey that should have taken eleven days had lasted forty years! And the reason for that was Israel's refusal to go in and take the land when the opportunity and command to do so was given them by God.

Deuteronomy 1:19-46 recalls the events at Kadesh Barnea, first described in Numbers 13—14. The bad report of ten of the spies sent out to reconnoiter the land sent the people into a tailspin of grumbling rebellion and inferiority complex. In a panic, they refused to go any further. It is in this context that Moses spoke the words quoted above. He appealed to their experience of God's provision so far, how God had rescued them from Egypt and then protected and provided for them in the wilderness. And in this, says Moses, the LORD carried you, just like a father carrying his son. Perhaps he has in mind the image of carrying that God himself had used:

> You yourselves have seen what I did to Egypt, and how I carried
> you on eagles' wings and brought you to myself. (Ex 19:4)

Moses simply transfers the transport from parent birds to parent humans. The point is the same—caring, strong, parental protection and support.

Unfortunately, our text goes on to say that even this was not enough to persuade the people. "In spite of this,"—that is, in spite of all their eyes had seen and all they had experienced of God's fatherly support—"you did not trust in the LORD your God" (Deut 1:32). And so they ended up in the wilderness for a whole generation—where they continued to experience God's fatherly action, though in a somewhat different way (as we shall see in a moment).

Another text uses the picture of God as the parental porter to great effect. In Isaiah 46, the prophet first pours scorn on the gods of Babylon. When their city falls, far from these gods being able to come down to rescue their *worshipers*, they can't even stoop down to rescue their own *statues!* So these "gods" have to be carried out of the city on oxcarts. What kind of god is that? is the implied question. By contrast, God says,

Listen to me, O house of Jacob
all you who remain of the house of Israel,
you whom I have upheld since you were conceived,
and have carried since your birth.
Even to your old age and gray hairs
I am he, I am he who will sustain you.
I have made you and I will carry you;
I will sustain you and I will rescue you (Is 46:3-4).

The text does not actually name God as Father, but it certainly has that picture in mind, since it speaks of God carrying Israel from birth. This is not, however, like a human father who at some point has to give up carrying his children—usually when they grow bigger than he is! God carries his people from the cradle to the grave. He is our maker, carrier, sustainer and rescuer (Is 46:4)—all supremely fatherly qualities.

The point of Moses' reference to God as the carrying Father was to urge the people to trust him in the future, since he had not failed them in the past. The point of Isaiah's similar language was to urge the people not to be intimidated by the dazzling gods of Babylon, which would soon have to be carted away by the very people they were supposed to protect. Rather they should trust in the God of their history, who had carried them all this way and would do so to the very end. Which would you prefer—a god you have to carry yourself when you most need him, or the God who carries you from start to finish? God the Fraud, or God the Father?

GOD—THE FATHER WHO DISCIPLINES

Remember how the LORD your God led you all the way in the desert these forty years, to humble you and to test you in order to know what was in your heart, whether or not you would keep his commands. He humbled you, causing you to hunger and then feeding you with manna, which neither you nor your fathers had known, to teach you that man does not live on bread alone but on every word that comes from the mouth of the LORD. Your clothes did not wear out and your feet did not swell during these forty years. Know then in your heart that *as a man disciplines his son, so the LORD your God disciplines you.* (Deut 8:2-5, italics added)

Moses is still writing his memoirs. The wilderness had not been entirely wasted time. It had been an education. In fact, it was a learning experience for God as well as for Israel. What God wanted to know was what was in the hearts of his people, and whether or not they would learn to obey him. Our text sounds somewhat like an experimental laboratory in which various tests are carried out to examine a new product. So the privations of the wilderness journey functioned to test and to teach. In that sense, they were disciplinary.

The word "discipline" does not simply mean punishment—even though there were occasions of that in the wilderness. Rather it means the necessary strictness, constraints, limitation and rigor that are essential for any kind of effective learning. In modern times we associate such discipline with the school or college environment, or any place of disciplined training. In Israel, education took place in the household and was the primary responsibility of the father. So, once again, God is compared to a father—a father who will allow his children to experience tough times and even severe challenges, precisely in order that they will learn from them, and a father who will not shrink from exercising all necessary dimensions of discipline to ensure that the learning takes place. Discipline, in this sense, is a very positive word, because of the results and blessings that flow from exercising it (on oneself), or being the willing object of it (on the part of God or one's father or teacher).

Such discipline is a function of parental love, and quite different, of course, from arbitrary domestic violence and excessive punishment that arises from sheer anger or brutality and produces alienation and despair. That is why the wise father figure depicted in Proverbs not only urges the younger learner repeatedly to respect the wisdom and authority of his earthly father and mother, but even more so, to welcome the loving discipline of the LORD.

> My son, do not despise the LORD's discipline
> and do not resent his rebuke,
> because *the LORD disciplines those he loves,*
> *as a father the son he delights in.* (Prov 3:11-12, italics added)

Jesus, of course, never received his Father's rebuke. But he was certainly the Son whom his Father loved and delighted in. And yet the New Testament makes it clear that Jesus too went through the disciplinary and testing dimension of suffering, and that his obedience was, in that sense, "learned." As Hebrews puts it: "Although he was a son, he learned obedience from what he suffered" (Heb 5:8). This does not mean that he had been disobedient before, but only that, for Jesus as well as for us, sonship, discipline and obedience were all linked together in his relationship with his Father.

In fact, it is hard to read Moses' account of Israel's forty years in the wilderness in Deuteronomy 8 (above), without thinking of Jesus' forty days in the wilderness. Try reading those verses from within the mind of Jesus as a way of understanding how he, Jesus, not only recognized the nature of the testing he was experiencing, but also found the scriptural resources to fight back against the devil's attempt to undermine his commitment to the costly way his Father planned for him. Jesus submitted to his Father's discipline in life, just as he willingly submitted to his Father's will in death, and in Gethsemane beforehand. In this, as in all else, Jesus models for us the true response to our heavenly Father—one of submission to his loving discipline. And it is a response which, as in so much of his life and teaching, Jesus learned from his Scriptures, the Old Testament, where this fatherly character of God is so effectively painted.

Hebrews, similarly soaked in Scriptural teaching, draws the verses from Proverbs into a moving exhortation that builds on the metaphorical transference to God of human fatherly functions and points to the positive results if only we recognize and submit to our Father in such times.

In your struggle against sin, you have not yet resisted to the point of shedding your blood. And you have forgotten that word of encouragement that addresses you as sons:

"My son, do not make light of the Lord's discipline,
and do not lose heart when he rebukes you,
because the Lord disciplines those he loves,
and he punishes everyone he accepts as a son."

Endure hardship as discipline; God is treating you as sons. For what son is not disciplined by his father? If you are not disciplined (and everyone undergoes discipline), then you are illegitimate children and not true sons. Moreover, we have all had human fathers who disciplined us and we respected them for it. How much more should we submit to the Father of our spirits and live! Our fathers disciplined us for a little while as they thought best; but God disciplines us for our good, that we may share in his holiness. No discipline seems pleasant at the time, but painful. Later on, however, it produces a harvest of righteousness and peace for those who have been trained by it. (Heb 12:4-11)

GOD—THE FATHER WHO PITIES

The LORD is compassionate and gracious,
   slow to anger, abounding in love.
He will not always accuse,
   nor will he harbor his anger forever;
he does not treat us as our sins deserve
   or repay us according to our iniquities.
For as high as the heavens are above the earth,
   so great is his love for those who fear him;
as far as the east is from the west,
   so far has he removed our transgressions from us.
As a father has compassion on his children,
   so the LORD has compassion on those who fear him;
for he knows how we are formed,
   he remembers that we are dust. (Psalm 103:8-14, italics added)

The best worship songs are those that are soaked in Scripture. The best sermons are those that expound the biblical text. Here we have a psalm that turns scriptural exposition into exquisite poetry. The psalmist's basic text is Exodus 34:6-7. This was God's declaration of his self-identity—given to Moses in the wake of the great apostasy of Israel at Mount Sinai, with the golden calf (in Exodus 32—34, which we will study in chapter three). It is a powerful statement of the character of God that echoes throughout the Bible in many forms.[1]

---

[1]It would be worth pausing to read the following texts to feel the force of these affirmations in many different moments of the life of God's people: Num 14:18; Deut 5:9-10; 1 Kings 3:6; Neh 9:17; Ps 86:15; 103:8, 17; 145:8; Jer 32:18-19; Lam 3:32; Dan 9:4; Jon 4:2; Nahum 1:3.

The psalmist, along with many Old Testament writers, marvels at the imbalance between the love and the anger of God. He does not, of course, minimize God's wrath—how could he with all the narratives of the Old Testament to reflect on?—but he does put it into a minor key compared with God's grace and compassion. God's love is abounding; his anger is slow—that is, it is often delayed in operation. His love, as so many Scriptures affirm, is eternal; his anger will not last forever. God fully recognizes our sins, iniquities and transgressions, but does not instantly treat us as they deserve. This is the quality of grace that the psalm as a whole celebrates.

The psalmist not only revels in the affirmation of Exodus 34:6 (in Ps 103:8):

The LORD, the LORD, the compassionate and gracious God, slow to anger, abounding in love and faithfulness; (Ex 34:6)

He also reflects on the first half of Exodus 34:7 (in Ps 103:10, 12):

maintaining love to thousands, and *forgiving wickedness, rebellion and sin.* (Ex 34:7, italics added)

For those last three words ("wickedness, rebellion and sin") are exactly the same three Hebrew words that the psalmist lists in Psalm 103:10 and 12. These are the things that deserve God's wrath, but God chooses *not* to "treat us according to them" (Ps 103:10, literally), but rather to "remove" them from us altogether (Ps 103:12).

Psalm 103 does not tell us why or how God can do this—only that he does, and is to be eternally thanked and praised for doing so. Exodus 34:7 actually says that God *"carries"* wickedness, rebellion and sin. He bears it (which the NIV translates as "forgiving"). Now this is interesting. Not only is this the same Hebrew word (*nasa'*) as is used in the section above for God "carrying" his people, it is also the same word that Isaiah uses about the Servant of the Lord in Isaiah 53. Whereas "we" (the unnamed observers) thought that the Servant of the Lord was undergoing all his sufferings because God was punishing him for his own sin, what we now realize, to our great surprise, is that it was actually *our* sins that he was *"carrying"*—and that he carried right through his flagrantly unjust trial and horrendously violent death.

> Surely he took up our infirmities
>   and *carried* our sorrows,
> yet we considered him stricken by God,
>   smitten by him, and afflicted.
> But he was pierced for our transgressions,
>   he was crushed for our iniquities;
> the punishment that brought us peace was upon him,
>   and by his wounds we are healed.
> We all, like sheep, have gone astray,
>   each of us has turned to his own way;
> and the LORD has *laid on him*
>   the iniquity of us all.
>
> Therefore I will give him a portion among the great,
>   and he will divide the spoils with the strong,
> because he poured out his life unto death,
>   and was numbered with the transgressors.
> For he *bore [carried]* the sin of many,
>   and made intercession for the transgressors.
> (Is 53:4-6, 12, italics added)

The author of Psalm 103 exalts the forgiving grace of God, in that God does not deal with us as our sins deserve, but he is careful to point out (though without further explanation) that this can happen only because God himself has "removed our transgressions from us." It is other Scriptures that show us how God did the removal: by carrying them himself, in the person of his Servant. Or as Peter would later express it, unquestionably reflecting on Isaiah 53 as he wrote the words, "He [Christ] himself bore our sins in his body on the tree, so that we might die to sins and live for righteousness; by his wounds you have been healed" (1 Pet 2:24).

Poets and preachers expand their root themes with richly suggestive metaphors. So here, the psalmist colors in the compassionate grace of God in dealing with our sins by means of three metaphors. The first two are spatial—height and breadth. God's love is as high as the heavens are above the earth. God's moving van has transported our sins as far away as the East is from the West. And the third is relational. In behaving thus, God is like a human father who feels pity and compassion (the Hebrew word contains both emotions) for his children in their small size and physical limitations. A good father does not expect his children to have the strength of adults, and he makes allowances for their frailty. God does not expect of us more than is humanly possible. This is not to say, of course, that our sin is excusable, or that God is not grieved and angered by our wickedness and rebellion. No Old Testament psalmist could have entertained such a thought. Rather it means, simply, that God is no less understanding of all our human limitations than any good father is of his children's vulnerability.

One might have expected the psalmist to illustrate his general point by reference back to the historical act of forgiveness that his main text comes from—the episode of the golden calf in Exodus 32—34. But instead, the fatherly comparison in Psalm 103:13 leads him right back to creation, and another text—Genesis 2:7: "The LORD God *formed* the man from the *dust* of the ground" (italics added). As we have said earlier, the Old Testament resists any idea that the fatherhood of God implied any physical, sexual or biological parenting of the human race by God. Humans are not the offspring of the gods in any literal sense. Nevertheless, God is as surely the "progenitor" of humanity, by having "formed" us, as any human father is of his children. And, just as a father knows when his children were born, so God "knows our forming and remembers that dust is what we are" (a literal rendering of the Hebrew in Ps 103:14). And in that remembering lies God's understanding of us and his fatherly compassion for us.

And in response to such fatherly factors in the character of God and in his attitude and action toward us, it is indeed right that we should summon up "all that is within us" to bless the Lord, and forget not all his benefits (Ps 103:1-2, author's translation).

GOD—THE FATHER WHO ADOPTS

Do not hide your face from me,
    do not turn your servant away in anger;
    you have been my helper.
Do not reject me or forsake me,
    O God my Savior.
Though my father and mother forsake me,
    the LORD *will receive me.* (Ps 27:9-10, italics added)

Sing to God, sing praise to his name,
    extol him who rides on the clouds—
his name is the LORD—
    and rejoice before him.
A father to the fatherless, a defender of widows,
    is God in his holy dwelling.

God sets the lonely in families,
  he leads forth the prisoners with singing;
  but the rebellious live in a sun-scorched land.
(Psalm 68:4-6, italics added)

These are the only other references to God in comparison with a
human father in the book of Psalms (apart from the direct address
to God as "my Father," in the mouth of the Davidic king, in Psalm
89:26). They have in common the idea that God will step in as an
adoptive father in circumstances where human parents have
either disowned their child, or have left him orphaned. God, as
Father, takes over where human fatherhood fails for one reason or
another.

Psalm 27 begins with strong notes of faith in God and the courage
it generates in the face of enemies. And it is clear that the author is
indeed surrounded by enemies and stands in great need of God's protection and provision. Psalm 27:7-9 suggests that under the pressure
of the danger that surrounds him, the author is desperate for some
reassurance from God that he will indeed be there for him and deliver
on his promises. It is unlikely that Psalm 27:10 means that the writer
has actually been literally disowned by his human parents. Rather, he
probably contemplates the pain of such a devastating disgrace hypo-
thetically as the worst possible exacerbation of his feeling of standing
alone against the world. If even his parents should turn against him!
But in turning to God, as he does through the whole psalm, he knows
he is turning to the one whose loving commitment to him is stronger
even than the strongest human bond of parent and child. God is the
Father whose protection will never be withdrawn, whose commitment will outlast all earthly fatherhood. God is the Father who, if
ever the believer should be left effectively fatherless, will adopt him

as his own and take him in (NIV "receive" is rather weak; the word means to take up, take in, gather in, or gather up).

Psalm 68, overall, is a psalm celebrating the mighty power of Yahweh as the victorious God of Israel's history. So Psalm 68:5-6 is a kind of counterpoint, celebrating the compassionate and relational nature of God alongside his enormous and triumphant strength.

God's special concern for the orphan and widow is well documented, of course, throughout the Law and the Prophets, in the wisdom tradition (as for example in Job's echo of this text in Job 29:12-16), and in narratives such as Elijah's temporary accommodation with the widow of Zarephath or the story of Ruth. But here the concept is expressed not merely in the form of commands to human action (to care for the orphan and widows), but in picturing Yahweh himself as the adoptive father who takes care of the orphan, and the defending advocate who represents the widow in court and sees that she gets justice.

It is striking that in one of the very few Old Testament texts that actually speak directly of God as "father," the prime focus is on God's loving, protecting and defending stance toward the weak and vulnerable in human society—as typified in the most vulnerable of all, orphaned children. God is Father to those who have lost the natural bonds of human protection, whether because of rejection, or because of natural bereavement.

These are texts which surely speak with powerful and moving relevance into our world, where many people who come to faith in Christ find themselves disowned and expelled by their human families—even sometimes killed by their own fathers, and where HIV-AIDS is generating orphans and widows at a staggering rate. Loss of family is a terrible and terrifying thing in any era. The knowledge of the fatherhood of God is a biblical truth that cannot be lightly or glibly substituted as a panacea, but certainly provides a framework of ultimate and eternal security for those who come to know and trust in their heavenly Father through saving faith in his Son.

CONCLUSION

For Israel then, knowing God included knowing certain dimensions of his character and actions that could best be expressed and reflected upon by comparison with human fatherhood (or in some cases, parenthood). The idea of God as Father was not allowed to degenerate into the kind of pagan mythology that distorted the good gift of human sexuality into a lurid parody of divine sexual antics as the origin of the human race. God had not "fathered" humans by any such means. And perhaps, as we said, this is the reason why in Old Testament times they were reluctant to refer to God simply as "God the Father," as a title. Nevertheless, having said that, it is clear that God had acted, and could be asked to act, in ways that found analogies in the behavior of the best human fathers.

Here is God, the Father who carries his people, protecting them through all dangers, and whom we can trust like a child in his father's arms.

Here is God, the Father who disciplines his people, but does so for their benefit and learning. The wise child will submit to such discipline, recognizing the love that motivates it.

Here is God, the Father who pities his people, remembering the simple fact of their dusty humanity from the day he formed them, and acts to carry away their sin so that it can be forgiven. Such fatherly compassion calls for our gratitude and praise.

Here is God, the Father who takes over where human fathers fail or fall, adopting those who trust in him so that they are fatherless no longer. And in that lies our eternal security.

Here is God, we can now add in the light of the New Testament, the One whom we can rightly come to know as God the Father through the fuller revelation of his Son, Jesus Christ.

There are many more dimensions to the full biblical doctrine of the Fatherhood of God, but I hope it is clear by now that, in knowing Yahweh their God, these Old Testament believers had a remarkably profound understanding of some of what it means to know God as Father.

2

Knowing God Through
Experience of His Grace

Knowing God starts with knowing what God has done for us out of his love and grace. Certainly that is where Israelites would have begun. If you had asked any devout Israelite, "How do you know God?" he or she would have sat down with you to tell you a long story—the story of God in action on behalf of his people, especially the story of the exodus. And at the end they would have said, "And that's how we know the LORD our God. That is who he is, and that is how we know him."

And in doing so, your Israelite friend would have been doing exactly what Moses did in the text we shall unpack in this chapter. For the whole point of their history, says Moses, was precisely so that Israel should indeed *know* the truth and reality of their God. As Moses urges the people of Israel to be faithful to God as they move forward into a challenging future, he reminds them of their remarkable past. It is a past filled with the grace of God in action. Just think of all that God had done for Israel . . .

Ask now about the former days, long before your time, from the day God created man on the earth; ask from one end of the heavens to the other. Has anything so great as this ever happened, or has anything like it ever been heard of? Has any other people heard the voice of God speaking out of fire, as you have, and lived? Has any god ever tried to take for himself one nation out of another nation, by testings, by miraculous signs and wonders, by war, by a mighty hand and an outstretched arm, or by great and awesome deeds, like all the things the LORD your God did for you in Egypt before your very eyes?

You were shown these things so that you might know that the LORD is God; besides him there is no other. From heaven he made you hear his voice to discipline you. On earth he showed you his great fire, and you heard his words from out of the fire. Because he loved your forefathers and chose their descendants after them, he brought you out of Egypt by his Presence and his great strength, to drive out before you nations greater and stronger than you and to bring you into their land to give it to you for your inheritance, as it is today.

Acknowledge and take to heart this day that the LORD is God in heaven above and on the earth below. There is no other. Keep his decrees and commands, which I am giving you today, so that it may go well with you and your children after you and that you may live long in the land the LORD your God gives you for all time. (Deut 4:32-40, italics added)

I have highlighted Deuteronomy 4:35 and 39 because they provide the focal point of the passage. Why had God done all that he had done for Israel? So that they should *know* him as the only God (Deut 4:35) What should they do then? *Know* him in their hearts (Deut 4:39)! "Acknowledge" is simply a variation in English on what is exactly the same verb in Hebrew, "know."

For Israel, knowing Yahweh as God was founded on their experience of his action in history. They knew something in their heads as the truth because of something they had experienced in their lives as a reality. Knowledge and experience go together here—combined around the person and action of God. It is important that we always keep the two together, since some people tend to go to extremes in emphasizing one or the other.

"Never mind doctrine," say some people, "just feel the presence and power of God in your experience."

"No, we must teach the truth that people should know and believe," others assert; "Experience is subjective and suspicious."

But we should not divide the two like this. In the Bible God gives his people unmistakable *experiential* proof of his presence; but then he immediately goes on to teach them the *truth* that they need to learn in their heads from such experience.

Let's think, then, about four things from this passage. Each of them is an aspect of Israel's experience of God's grace and each of them relates to what it means to know God.

- the uniqueness of the experience
- the content of the experience
- the transmission of the experience
- the purpose of the experience

THE UNIQUENESS OF THE EXPERIENCE

Moses challenges the listening Israelites to reflect on their actual experience up to this point in their history. It is important also to recall that he is talking to people for whom this was actual historical experience. He is talking to the generation who were the children of those who had come out of Egypt in the exodus. They had been there with their parents at Mount Sinai. These were recent events in living memory. So Moses is not asking if they remember some ancient myths and legends, or if they can repeat the religious speculations of some great ancestor. He is asking them to recall things that had happened "before your very eyes" (Deut 4:34). This is historical reality, not religious mythology. That is where our knowledge of God is rooted.

Moses asks some grand questions in Deuteronomy 4:32-34. They are rhetorical questions—that is to say, he is not asking for information, but making an emphatic point. He imagines a research project of cosmic scale in Deuteronomy 4:32—taking in the whole universe of space and the whole history of time. Even in such a vast field of enquiry, will anybody come up with anything that could be compared with what God had just done for Israel through the exodus and at Sinai? The answer expected, of course, is, No, there is nothing like these things. Nothing like them has ever happened. What God did in bringing Israel out of slavery in Egypt and in speaking to them at Sinai was unique. And it was unique in two ways: it was unprecedented (God had never done such a thing at any other time), and it was unparalleled (God had never done such a thing anywhere else for any other nation).

Now we need to say at once that this does not imply that God was not interested in, or not involved in, the histories of other peoples. The Old Testament affirms again and again that Yahweh is the sovereign Lord of all nations on the planet and is active in all human history—not just the story of Israel. In fact, just a couple of chapters earlier this book of Deuteronomy has already made that point, in affirming that it was Yahweh who had moved many of the other nations around the lands of the Middle East in the same way that he was now moving Israel into possession of Canaan (Deut 2 as a whole, but see especially Deut 2:5, 9, 10-12, 19, 20-23). But in Israel alone God had been working for his unique purposes of salvation and covenant, and within his overall mission of bringing blessing ultimately to all nations, in fulfillment of his promise to Abraham. In this sense, God did in the history of Israel what he did nowhere else and "no-when" else.

So there is a uniqueness about Israel's experience of God that is being very powerfully affirmed here. Yahweh their God had redeemed them in a way that no other people had known (cf. Amos 3:1-2). And Yahweh had spoken to them in a way that no other people had ever heard (cf. Ps 147:19-20). And in both dimensions, God acted in his grace. The story of the exodus is presented as monumental proof of God's loving concern for his oppressed people and his faithfulness to his promise to Abraham. Love and faithfulness are both dimensions of God's grace. And the story of Sinai is presented as God, in all his awesome holiness, graciously entering into a covenant relationship with people who repeatedly prove themselves utterly unworthy of it. These were unique moments in all human history, and those who experienced them were experiencing the grace of the living God in action, grace that saved them out of slavery, grace that invited them into relationship. To know God through such experience was to know the God of grace.

THE CONTENT OF THE EXPERIENCE

We need to look in somewhat greater depth at these two aspects of Israel's experience that Moses highlights here. In fact he refers to each of them twice over in our passage, clearly intending to underline them by such repetition. They are:

The revelation at Mount Sinai (Deut 4:33, 36)

The redemption out of Egypt (Deut 4:34, 37—with the conquest also in view in Deut 4:38)

Both of these were primary experiences through which Israel came to know God. And both of them also have New Testament counterparts which relate to us and *our* experience of God, through which we too come to know him.

Revelation.

1. *The revelation of God at Sinai.* The primary account of what happened at Sinai is found in Exodus 19, and would be worth reading at this point, along with the interesting recollection of it in Deuteronomy 5. It was a staggeringly awesome audio-visual experience of the presence and power of God, and it burned itself into the collective memory of Israel for ever after. When you really needed to invoke the power of God, calling on him as the God of Sinai was the way to do it (Ps 68:8). Sinai was the greatest of all the Old Testament theophanies. *Theophany* means the appearing of God. At Sinai, God was heard (in the sound of thunder, the trumpet and the voice), felt (in an earthquake) and seen (in smoke and fire). He was not seen literally, of course, as Deuteronomy 4 has already carefully pointed out.

> Then the LORD spoke to you out of the fire. You heard the sound of words but saw no form; there was only a voice. (Deut 4:12)

> On earth he showed you his great fire, and you heard his words from out of the fire. (Deut 4:36)

But this was precisely the point. God encountered Israel at Sinai, not just to dazzle them with some spectacular cosmic fireworks, but to address them. He spoke words to them. That is, Sinai was an experience of intelligible, meaningful communication. God had things to say. Israel had things to understand. "The words," of course, meant first of all the so-called Ten Words—i.e., the Ten Commandments, the Decalogue. But that was certainly not the limit of God's communication at Sinai.

Already, at the burning bush encounter on Mount Sinai, God had revealed his personal name, Yahweh, to Moses, and this now becomes the focal point of all his revelation to the Israelites when they get there, too. "I am the LORD your God," is how the Ten Words begin (Deut 5:6). So at Sinai God revealed his own *identity*. At Sinai too he revealed his *character* as the God of grace and compassion, even in the teeth of Israel's rebellion.

> And he passed in front of Moses, proclaiming, "The LORD, the LORD, the compassionate and gracious God, slow to anger, abounding in love and faithfulness, maintaining love to thousands, and forgiving wickedness, rebellion and sin. Yet he does not leave the guilty unpunished; he punishes the children and their children for the sin of the fathers to the third and fourth generation." (Ex 34:6-7)

At Sinai, God revealed his *law*, his *covenant*, his *expectations* of Israel's *worship*—everything, in fact, that was needed to initiate and foster the relationship between God and this people that was so critical to God's ultimate plans for the world. All this God revealed at Sinai.

It only makes sense to talk about "knowing God" if it is actually possible for God to be known. There are religions and philosophies which do not accept such a possibility. In the Hindu worldview, for example, the transcendent divine being is ultimately unknowable. The Bible insists throughout that the living God of whom it speaks not only *can* be known, but *wills* to be known. And far from leaving it up to us to get to know him through some game of religious hide and seek, this God takes the initiative in revealing himself to us. God can be known because God has spoken.

Now of course we realize that we cannot *grasp* all there is to God. We cannot, in that sense, comprehend God fully. But to say that we, as finite creatures, cannot know *everything* in the infinity of God, is not to say that there is *nothing* we can confidently claim to know about God. It does not reduce everything about God to mystery, ambiguity or just a matter of opinion. We can truly know what God has said about himself.

It is also true that God has chosen not to reveal everything to us— there are some things he has kept to himself, as Deuteronomy 29 says.

> The secret things belong to the LORD our God, but the things revealed belong to us and to our children forever, that we may follow all the words of this law. (Deut 29:29)

What God *has* chosen to reveal to us of himself, however, is clear and intelligible, for he has spoken, in words of human language, for that very purpose.

> For this is what the LORD says—he who created the heavens, he is God; he who fashioned and made the earth, he founded it; he did not create it to be empty, but formed it to be inhabited—he says: "I am the LORD, and there is no other. I have not spoken in secret, from somewhere in a land of darkness; I have not said to Jacob's descendants, 'Seek me in vain.' I, the LORD, speak the truth; I declare what is right." (Is 45:18-19)

So it is not arrogant to claim that we know God, in relation to what he has revealed through his word. God has made himself known. God wills to be known. Indeed, Israel had been told that one of the underlying purposes for which God was acting to deliver them from oppression in Egypt was that they *would* know him (Ex 6:6-8).

2. *The revelation of God in Christ.* For us, however, living on this side of the coming of Jesus Christ and the New Testament, the opportunity and scope for knowing God through his revelation is vastly greater than anything available to the Israelites even in the wake of their experience at Sinai. The words they heard came from the Living God, and in that sense also from the living Word of God. But in Jesus

the Word became flesh and made his dwelling among us. We have seen his glory, the glory of the One and Only, who came from the Father, full of grace and truth. (Jn 1:14)

Or as the writer to the Hebrews put it,

In the past God spoke to our forefathers through the prophets at many times and in various ways, but in these last days he has spoken to us by his Son, whom he appointed heir of all things, and through whom he made the universe. (Heb 1:1-2)

Once again we notice the emphasis in these New Testament texts on historical facts, experienced and witnessed by those who knew Jesus. The God who spoke at Sinai delivered his final word in Bethlehem, in Galilee and in Jerusalem—in the person of his own Son, Jesus of Nazareth. And Jesus then entrusted his own words to his disciples, and through the gift of his Holy Spirit of truth, commissioned them to teach that truth with apostolic authority to the church for all coming generations including our own.

So, just as knowing God meant, for Israel, first knowing his revealed word given to them at Sinai, similarly for us, knowing God means knowing the revealed Word of God through Christ. Knowing God is a process that starts from God's side, from what God has done and said to make himself known. Our responsibility is to hear and heed. To know God is to know him as Revealer.

Redemption.

1. The exodus. The events that Moses speaks of in Deuteronomy 4:34 and 37 are of course those referred to in the first fifteen chapters of the book of Exodus. He does not explicitly describe them as "redemption" here, but he certainly did in the Song of Moses immediately after the event. In fact, Exodus 15 is the first time God is described as "redeeming" his people.

> In your unfailing love you will lead the people you
>   have redeemed.
> In your strength you will guide them to your holy dwelling.
>   (Ex 15:13)

The exodus is the first great act of God's redemption in the Old Testament, and the second greatest in the whole Bible—second only to the cross of Christ, which is spoken of in the New Testament as the "exodus he accomplished in Jerusalem" (Lk 9:31, author's translation). It was also an utterly comprehensive act in which God demonstrated the full extent of his redeeming love and power. Think of all the dimensions of Israel's bondage in Egypt.

- They were *politically* oppressed as an ethic immigrant minority, vulnerable to the host state's manufactured hostility against them.

- They were *economically* exploited as a convenient source of cheap labor in the host state's agricultural and construction sectors.

- They were *socially* victimized through intolerable interference in their family life and then through a program of state-sponsored genocide. The description of their plight in Exodus 1 has some very modern echoes.

- On top of all that, they were *spiritually* oppressed in servitude to the Pharaoh—one of the claimed gods of Egypt—when they should have been free to serve and worship Yahweh.

In the chain of events we call the exodus, God accomplished deliverance for them in all four areas. They were released from political injustice, from economic exploitation and from social violence. And they were released into covenant relationship with Yahweh their God at Sinai. The exodus, in other words, was an act of holistic redemption that transformed every dimension of Israel's holistic need. As such it stands as a prime biblical model of what God means by redemption, and what our missional response needs to take into account.[1]

In our text here, Moses picks out two major items in the catalog of what the exodus proved about God (we shall think of some more in the next chapter).

- On the one hand, his immense *power* that was demonstrated in his *victory* over his enemy (Deut 4:34).

- And on the other hand, his great *love and faithfulness* in fulfilling the promise he made to Israel's ancestors (Deut 4:37).

His great power and love are combined in his "Presence" (Deut 4:37), which is literally, his "Face." Israel's experience of the exodus was, in other words, an experience of the Face of God—even though they did not see his face in a literal sense. His actions of power and love on their behalf proved his personal presence in their midst. In these things, therefore, they had come to know him, to recognize him—just as we know someone through their face. It is another highly personal metaphor for knowing God.

2. *The cross.* Just as we have the revealing word of God embodied for us in the person of Jesus, so we have the great redeeming work

---

[1] I have discussed the exodus as a model of redemption and its significance for holistic mission more fully in *The Mission of God* (Downers Grove, Ill.: InterVarsity Press, 2006), chap. 8.

of God achieved for us by Jesus, through his atoning death on the cross. And amidst all the volumes we could now say about what we know of God because of the cross, we can simply pick out the same two features that match what Moses said about the exodus. For the New Testament likewise emphasizes the cross as the climactic demonstration of *God's power and his final victory* over all his enemies and over all that wrecks and spoils human life. The cross is the power of God in action.

> Having disarmed the powers and authorities, he made a public spectacle of them, triumphing over them by the cross. (Col 2:15)

And the cross is the ultimate proof of *God's love and faithfulness*.

> God demonstrates his own love for us in this: While we were still sinners, Christ died for us. (Rom 5:8)

To know God, then, is to know him as Redeemer, as Savior and Deliverer. It is to know the exodus God, Yahweh, the great I AM. It is to know the Calvary God, Jesus, "the Son of God, who loved me and gave himself for me," as Paul delighted to say (Gal 2:20).

All of this, then, happened in history, in reality, in experience. These were unique and unrepeatable events, in which God acted in revelation and redemption. This is how God has made himself known; and therefore this is how we are to know God. This is the claim and affirmation that Moses is making in our text, and that we rightly appropriate through our wider knowledge of the revealing and redeeming God from the New Testament. We come to know God through experience of his grace in action.

But this raises a question. Moses is here describing a unique historical experience that happened to a particular group of people in one generation, and could be recalled as a living experience at the most only by the younger generation—the children whom he now addresses as adults. How could later generations come to know God if they could not have that same experience? Moses says that the Israelites know God because these things happened before their very eyes. So what about later generations who weren't there to see it with their eyes? This leads us to reflect on our next point.

THE TRANSMISSION OF THE EXPERIENCE

The same question could be asked about Jesus and the cross as well, of course. It was all very well for those who were privileged to know him, who heard his teaching and watched his life, who witnessed his death and resurrection. Of course *they* knew him, and knew God through him. But what about all those who came later? Clearly Jesus himself pondered this issue, prepared for it (Jn 14:15-18, 25-26; 16:12-16), prayed about it (Jn 17:20), and promised even greater blessing to those who would believe without having "been there" to see what the disciples saw (Jn 20:29).

We have been saying that we come to know God through the experience of his grace. How does that happen? Well, for two generations in history, it happened by actually being there and witnessing God's grace in action (the Israelites who experienced the exodus; and the disciples who saw Jesus' life, death and resurrection). For the rest of us (whether subsequent generations of Israelites in the Old Testament, or generations of Christian believers ever since the first century), there are three ways at least in which that primary historical experience also becomes ours, and thereby becomes the means of our knowing God: through telling the story and teaching the faith; through the inspired Scriptures, and through the sacramental reenactment of the events themselves.

Telling and teaching. Again and again in Deuteronomy Moses urges the Israelites to make sure that the story was regularly told and its significance thoroughly taught to all subsequent generations.

> Only be careful, and watch yourselves closely so that you do not forget the things your eyes have seen or let them slip from your heart as long as you live. Teach them to your children and to their children after them. (Deut 4:9; cf. 6:4-9, 20-25)

Israel was a community of memory. They were to preserve the knowledge of God by constantly re-telling the story of the acts of God. Conversely, if they failed to do so, they both "forgot God," and lost their knowledge of God—with disastrous results, as the prophets testify.

The Scriptures. The oral re-telling of the story was essential, and was to form part of every family's instruction so as to enable each generation to relive the events and enter into the experience of God's grace that they contained. But God's purpose was also to have a written record that would supplement and where necessary correct human memory, and provide a permanent witness of all that he had said and done. And so we have the Scriptures—breathed out by God, as Paul said (2 Tim 3:16), while at the same time entirely written by human authors.

Deuteronomy, yet again, sees the need for this written record alongside the oral telling and teaching, and makes clear provision for it. The book of Deuteronomy itself, of course, is one example of the very thing it is talking about.

> So Moses wrote down this law and gave it to the priests, the sons of Levi, who carried the ark of the covenant of the LORD, and to all the elders of Israel. Then Moses commanded them: "At the end of every seven years, in the year for canceling debts, during the Feast of Tabernacles, when all Israel comes to appear

before the LORD your God at the place he will choose, you shall read this law before them in their hearing. Assemble the people—men, women and children, and the aliens living in your towns—so they can listen and learn to fear the LORD your God and follow carefully all the words of this law. Their children, who do not know this law, must hear it and learn to fear the LORD your God as long as you live in the land you are crossing the Jordan to possess." (Deut 31:9-13)

If we look at some of the great revivals of faith that took place in the course of Israel's history, they included this element of the reading of the written Word of God, so that people could enter again into that experience of God which would lead them to repentance, but also to rejoicing and obedience (e.g., Josiah in 2 Kings 22—23, and Ezra in Neh 8). Likewise for Timothy, Paul observes that it was the faithful reading and teaching of the Scriptures that had led Timothy to saving faith in Christ and ethical instruction (2 Tim 3:14-16).

We can never stress too much the importance of the Scriptures in knowing God, even when we rightly talk about knowing God being a matter of experience. For when we say that we know God through experience of his grace, we are not talking merely about some subjective, inward or mystical personal experience. The emphasis is not just on experience for its own sake, without regard for content or control. Knowing God means entering into a *biblically informed* experience. It means entering into *this* story, as it is told in the Bible. It means engaging with the Scriptural interpretation of what the story means, and what it reveals of the words and works of God. If we cut loose from the Scriptures and allow any so-called experience of God to be treated as valid knowledge of God, then we can end up in dangerous waters without a rudder or an anchor.

This affects our mission and evangelism also. We long to bring people to know God. That is surely one of our primary evangelistic goals. But we must make sure that it is the God of the Bible they are coming to know. So at some point in the whole process of bringing people to faith, and then to discipleship, we must lead them to the Scriptures, so that their own personal experience of God's grace will be biblically informed and authenticated. They need to know this story—the grand narrative of the whole Bible (not in every detail at first, of course, but in its over-arching structural unity). Here is The Story of God and the world, of humanity's dignity and depravity, of where we are and who we are, of what's gone wrong and what God has done to put things right, of where it will all end and where we are headed for. Only within this grand narrative can we know God truly, through experiencing his grace in action through these great events.

If people are to come to know God, then they must know these great biblical realities, enshrined in the great biblical story. This is clear in both the Old and New Testaments. So, for example, when the psalmists contemplated how the nations would eventually come to know and worship Yahweh—the God of Israel but also the only true and living God—they saw it as a matter of proclaiming among the nations the great story of God's mighty acts in Israel through which the name, salvation and glory of Yahweh God had been revealed.

> Sing to the LORD a new song;
>   sing to the LORD, all the earth.
> Sing to the LORD, praise his *name;*
>   proclaim his *salvation* day after day.
> Declare his *glory* among the nations,
>   his *marvelous deeds* among all peoples.
> (Ps 96:1-3, italics added)

And among the key tasks that Jesus laid upon his apostles in their task of making disciples of all nations was "teaching them to obey everything I have commanded you" (Matt 28:20).

The sacraments. So the story is to be told and taught; the Scriptures are to be read and taught. But in addition, and in both Testaments, God provided for a practical reenactment of the historical events in which his redeeming grace had been so powerfully operating, so that by engaging in these regular actions the people of God would not only preserve the memory of the original events but continue to enter into the experience of grace that they embodied. We are talking about the Passover and the Lord's Supper.

Both of these are "memorials." That is to say, they function as reminders of the events they celebrate: the exodus and the death of Christ respectively. And that, as we have seen, is an important thing in itself. The people of God must remember, remember, remember, in order to know God through his great acts. But they are more than just memorials. When Jews and Christians celebrate the Passover and the Lord's Supper, it is as if they enter a kind of two-way time machine in relation to those events.

1. The sacraments locate us "as if we were there." Every generation of Israelites recited the words of Deuteronomy 6:21 (italics added), "*We* were slaves of Pharaoh in Egypt, but the LORD brought *us* out of Egypt with a mighty hand." They put themselves in the shoes of the oppressed Hebrews, and in the Passover meal they enter again into the experience of the slavery, the plagues and the nighttime deliverance. They relive the story as if it were their own—which by faith and corporate identification, it is. Likewise, at every Holy Communion service, the Christian hears the words of Christ, spoken first to the disciples, but now addressed to him or her, "This is my body given for *you*; this is the cup of the new covenant in my blood, which is shed for you, and for many." The story, the actions, the words, put us in that room with Jesus on the night he was betrayed. There is an old spiritual that asks the repeated question, "Were you there when they crucified my Lord?" Spiritually speaking, by faith and in sacramental action, the answer is Yes. Of course, this is not implying that the actions of the Holy Communion are in any sense a repetition of the sacrifice of Christ. As the Anglican liturgy makes clear, we celebrate his one, perfect and sufficient sacrifice, made once for all on the cross. But it does mean that we see ourselves as witnesses and beneficiaries of what Christ did. We were there. It was for us. The cross was a unique historical event, but the sacrament connects us to it by the sanctified imagination of faith and gratitude.

2. *The sacraments present the events "as if now."* If, on the one hand, participation in the sacrament puts us back in time to the original historical events, so, on the other hand, such participation brings the event right up into our present, as if it were happening for us now. The Israelites celebrate again the saving power of the God who is always present with them in times of need and oppression—or indeed cry out to him to do again what he did for them in delivering them from Egypt. The Christian receives once again the grace and forgiveness that flow from the cross, the cleansing power of the blood of Christ. And as the bread is broken and eaten and the wine poured out and drunk, as it was on that night two thousand years ago, we "feed on him in our hearts by faith, with thanksgiving," here and now, in the present. The *act* of grace was that unrepeatable historical event. The *means* of grace is the repeated experience of receiving it by faith and absorbing its benefits in our whole lives.

Knowing God, then, is a matter of experiencing God's grace—for Israel and for us. And of course, for each individual that has to be a personal, inward and unique experience. Each one of us must know

God for ourselves as the unique person God has made us to be. Nobody's testimony of their knowledge of God is identical to anyone else's. And yet, it is important to stress, on the basis of the last three points, that knowing God is also a shared and collective experience. To know God I must join myself with those who experienced the original events of God's revelation and salvation. I put myself alongside them by faith and so join the great historical "communion of saints" of every generation. And at the same time, I join the great company of those around me in the present who also share this experience, reflect upon it in the light of Scripture, and celebrate it in the presence of God.

Knowing God, then, to amplify a point made above, is not some private, esoteric devotional state of mind or heart. Nor is it "whatever I make of it"—just so long as "me and God" get along fine together. There are some kinds of popular "spiritualities," and some kinds of devotional literature, which pander to this form of self-obsession. For that is really what it is. "Knowing God" can become just another handy item in my inventory of self-fulfillment techniques. God becomes adjectival to my persona, an accessory to my self-esteem. As against all such narcissism, the Bible insists that knowing God starts out from who God is and what God has done—meaning what he did a very long time before we ever came along. To know him we must join ourselves to that great heritage of historical faith and memory, enter into these stories, and experience the grace of God in them, along with the company of all God's people.

Knowing God is not an exercise in getting God to fit into my life. Knowing God is an exercise in humbly fitting myself into God's great historical story of redemptive grace.

But for what purpose? Why did these great unique historical events take place at all, and what was it that Israel was to learn in particular in the experience of knowing God through them. That leads us, then, fourth, to:

THE PURPOSE OF THE EXPERIENCE

Our two key verses come back into sharp focus at this point.

> You were shown these things so that you might know that the LORD is God; besides him there is no other. (Deut 4:35)

> Acknowledge and take to heart this day that the LORD is God in heaven above and on the earth below. There is no other. (Deut 4:39)

"So that you might know . . ." Israel's experience of the revealing and redeeming grace of God was intended to be educational. They were to learn something from it about Yahweh as God. What was that? Well, obviously, they were to learn all that had already been said in the previous verses about Yahweh. Look at those verses again and see in them some of the rudiments of Israel's knowledge of God. They now know that Yahweh is the God who speaks, who disciplines, who loves, who keeps his promises, who is a miraculous deliverer and powerful victor over his enemies. In the next chapter we shall look at some of these and more in Israel's curriculum of knowing their God.

But what verses 35 and 39 stress above and beyond all these truths is the universality and uniqueness of Yahweh as God. He is God "in heaven above and on the earth below"—that is, he fills the whole cosmos. There is nowhere else to be God in. Yahweh is the universal God—not just the national god of little Israel. And "there is no other." He is unique because he is the only. This is affirming much more than that Yahweh was the only God that Israel was to worship (while allowing for the existence of other gods of other nations). It is hard to read it as anything other than a statement of the transcendent uniqueness of Yahweh as the only living God in the universe.

So here we have an uncompromisingly monotheistic affirmation. But it is not expressed in the way we might expect, as if monotheism *per se* were all that the Israelites were supposed to deduce from their experience. Moses did not say, "You were shown these things so that you would know that there is only one God." If he had, one might imagine James muttering back, "You believe that there is one God? Good! Even the demons believe that—and shudder" (Jas 2:19). Monotheism as mere arithmetic doesn't get you very far. No, the point is not so much the singularity of deity (as it is in Deut 6:4-5), but the identity of deity. The question is "Who is God? Who is Lord?" This text answers, Yahweh alone is God. And the New Testament adds, Jesus alone is Lord—and (in both cases), "there is no other." No other God than Yahweh. No other name by which we must be saved, than the name of Jesus. God is as he is revealed in Yahweh. God is as he is revealed in Jesus. The only God who saves is Yahweh. The only one through whom God saves is Jesus.

These are the great affirmations that are involved in knowing God, in the way that this text and those that echo it demand. This is what we must "acknowledge and take to heart," in the task of knowing God through the experience of his grace. To know God is to know the living, biblical God of revelation and redemption, experienced through these events—not some figment of our own imagination, or the myths of our culture, or the masquerading gods of the idolatries that surround us.

And as we choose to know this God in this way, then the final command of this passage swims across the horizon into sharp focus.

Keep his decrees and commands, which I am giving you today,
so that it may go well with you and your children after you.
(Deut 4:40)

If this is the God we are called to know, then he is also the God we
are called to obey. Indeed, as we shall see in a later study, to know
God is to obey him.

3

Knowing God Through
Exposure to His Judgment

Grace comes first. In chapter two we saw that for us to know God at all is a matter of the grace of God. But more than that, we come to know him as we witness his grace in action and experience it for ourselves. And that is what God wants, since he told the Israelites that the purpose for which they had experienced the great redeeming and revealing work of God in their history was so that they would know him to be the only living God. And we saw that the same principle holds good for us as Christian believers also. We know God when we experience God in action.

But "God in action" cuts more than one way. The exodus was a great deliverance for the Israelites. But it was at the same time a great judgment upon the Egyptians who had oppressed them. It is presented as the paradigmatic act of God's justice, so celebrated in the Bible, by which he vindicates and liberates the downtrodden, and condemns the oppressor. So in the exodus, the release of the Hebrew slaves required the overthrow of the power that held them captive—the Pharaoh. It did not have to be that way, as the story tells how God through Moses asked Pharaoh voluntarily to do justice, stop the oppression and let the Israelites go. But he refused. Not once, but again. And again and again. And again and again and again, as the narrative piles up the pressure of the conflict of wills between Yahweh and

Pharaoh. In the end, however, the outcome is inevitable.

And apart from the obvious outcome that the *Israelites* were released, and thereby came to know the God they were dealing with, the story is at pains to make the balancing point that *Pharaoh* too came to know God. Or to be more precise, Pharaoh came to know that Yahweh, the God he refused to acknowledge, was indeed God—more powerful than himself, his magicians or any of the gods of Egypt. Knowing God, then, is not a sweet and cozy inner feeling. It is an encounter with the supreme governor of history, and its outcome depends entirely on the stance you adopt in relation to him. Israel came to know God as Savior. Pharaoh came to know God as judge. In this chapter we will look at the content of this dual educational encounter, starting with Pharaoh.

THE GOD PHARAOH CAME TO KNOW

The pupil—a man who refused to know God. The trigger for the great power encounter between Yahweh and Pharaoh begins with Pharaoh's refusal to even recognize the name of the God in whose name Moses was making his request.

> Afterward Moses and Aaron went to Pharaoh and said, "This is what the LORD, the God of Israel, says: 'Let my people go, so that they may hold a festival to me in the desert.'" Pharaoh said, "Who is the LORD, that I should obey him and let Israel go? I do not know the LORD and I will not let Israel go." (Ex 5:1-2)

Remember, "the LORD" means the personal name of Yahweh. Pharaoh's astonishingly foolhardy answer says, in effect, "Excuse me? Who did you say? Who is this god you are talking of? 'Yahweh'—who is that? I do not recognize any god by that name in this realm. We have our own gods in Egypt, and I am one of them. I am under no obligation to take instructions from whatever god you are claiming to represent."

You can almost hear the sharp intake of breath among the angels. "You don't want to say that, friend. You will know who this God is by the time he has finished with you."

And that indeed becomes a major theme in the chapters that follow. It's easy to see that the chapters of Exodus 1—15 are all about the exodus. But the subplot underneath is that this story is all about knowing God. It is about a man who claimed he did not and would not "know" this God and how he was brought to exactly that knowledge, but only when it was too late.

The curriculum—what Pharaoh had to learn. After the encounter between Pharaoh, Moses and Aaron had gone so disastrously wrong in Exodus 5, God renews his promise that he will, without any doubt, bring the Israelites out. And he pointedly emphasizes that in the process *they* will know who he is, even if Pharaoh refuses to (Ex 6:2-8). Unfortunately the Israelites were almost as unimpressed as Pharaoh at that stage, and even Moses thinks God needs to be more realistic (Ex 6:12). There is a lot of learning to be done on all sides in this narrative.

As the story resumes in Exodus 7, the phrase "then you (or they) will know," or a variant of it, occurs in every chapter from Exodus 7—11 and then again in Exodus 14. All of them except two (10:2; 11:7) refer to Pharaoh or the Egyptians. Altogether the phrase comes thirteen times in these chapters. That is why it is right to include this whole episode in our study of "knowing God through the Old Testament." It may not be quite the kind of knowing God that we envisaged, or that we would like to add to our devotional checklist, but it is clearly an emphatic theme in the whole narrative. God intends that, like it or not, Pharaoh will *know* him and know a significant quantity of theological truth about him, even if he hardens his heart against the knowledge he accumulates so painfully, to his own final destruction. This is a portion of the Bible that has a major interest in what it means to know God.

What then was on the curriculum for Pharaoh? Let's survey the sequence of lessons.

1. *That Yahweh is truly God.*

And the Egyptians will know that I am the LORD when I stretch out my hand against Egypt and bring the Israelites out of it. . . . This is what the LORD says: By this you will know that I am the LORD: With the staff that is in my hand I will strike the water of the Nile, and it will be changed into blood. (Ex 7:5, 17)

This is the simplest starting point. Pharaoh had refused to acknowledge that Yahweh was a god at all, or at any rate one that he needed to take any notice of, let alone obey. The first two plagues demonstrate the reality of Yahweh's existence and divine power. God starts with the easier things first, as it were, since Pharaoh's magicians manage to replicate the trick with the staff and turning the Nile to blood (though I have often thought they would have served their king better if they had found a spell in their books marked, "Blood, how to turn back to water").

2. *That Yahweh has no rivals.*

Moses replied, "It will be as you say, so that you may know there is no one like the LORD our God. The frogs will leave you and your houses, your officials and your people; they will remain only in the Nile." (Ex 8:10-11)

Here the point is not merely that Yahweh is to be counted among the gods (from Pharaoh's perspective), but that he is in fact unique among them (if Pharaoh wants to be comparative). There is no God like Yahweh. He has no rivals or peers. This is language that will reverberate throughout the Old Testament in many other contexts. We shall return to it as part of Israel's learning curriculum below.

By this time, Pharaoh's magicians have run out of steam. Not only can they not keep up with the demonstrations of Yahweh's power, they are now very keen to acknowledge for themselves that a pretty powerful God is at work here—even if they failed to persuade Pharaoh to agree (Ex 8:19).

3. *That Yahweh is God in Egypt.*

On that day I will deal differently with the land of Goshen, where my people live; no swarms of flies will be there, so that you will know that I, the LORD, am in this land. I will make a distinction between my people and your people. This miraculous sign will occur tomorrow. (Ex 8:22-23)

The land of Goshen had been given to the Israelites by a previous Pharaoh several generations earlier. The gift of land to a group of famine refugees at that time had been an act of the Pharaoh's sovereign authority over the land as a whole. But if the present Pharaoh thought that he was really god in the land of Egypt he was about to learn another lesson. This Yahweh was not merely the god of the despised ethnic minority Pharaoh was so mercilessly exploiting; he was in fact God throughout the whole land of Egypt and had the power to distinguish one part of it from another. Yahweh is not just in Goshen. He is "in this land"—i.e., this land of Egypt, this domain of Pharaoh, as a whole.

4. That Yahweh is God of all the earth.

Let my people go, so that they may worship me, or this time I will send the full force of my plagues against you and against your officials and your people, so you may know that there is no one like me in all the earth. For by now I could have stretched out my hand and struck you and your people with a plague that would have wiped you off the earth. But I have raised you up for this very purpose, that I might show you my power and that my name might be proclaimed in all the earth. (Ex 9:13-16)

This is clearly an expansion on the previous statement. Yahweh is not only God in the land of Egypt, but he is beyond compare "in all the earth." This passage is also the central climax of all these "knowing" statements in the context. Not only does it reaffirm what God has been repeatedly trying to get Pharaoh to acknowledge— namely that Yahweh is God, that he has enormous power, and that he has no equals; it also affirms, for the first time, God's wider educational purpose in this whole sequence of events. And that is not confined to a demonstration of his power to this pigheaded king. No, there is a universal intent. God wills to be known "in all the earth," and this event will be one of the means by which that will happen. As indeed it has. For the exodus story is but one part of the whole Bible narrative of the saving acts of God, culminating in the cross and resurrection of his Son, Jesus Christ. So wherever that greater story is told, the name of the living God of the exodus is proclaimed.

The irony here is also very stark. This Pharaoh refused to acknowledge the name of Yahweh as God. But we do not even know for sure what *his* name was! The word "Pharaoh" is not a personal name; it is a title, like "King." And historians still dispute exactly which of the many Pharaohs of Egypt was the Pharaoh of the exodus (depending on which century the exodus is dated, and there are various theories). But God says to him, "I have raised you up" (as God does for all kings), "not so that everybody will know who *you* were when you've gone, but so that everybody will know who *I* am. *Your name* will be lost to history. *My name* will be known in all the earth."

5. *That Yahweh is judge of all supposed gods.*

> On that same night I will pass through Egypt and strike down every firstborn—both men and animals—and I will bring judgment on all the gods of Egypt. I am the LORD. (Ex 12:12)

This is not strictly in the sequence of "then you will know" texts. But it certainly adds to the knowledge of God contained in this narrative. The climactic tenth plague that will finally bring Pharaoh and all his people to beg the Israelites to leave is about to be unleashed. But this verse gives us one of several clues that this contest has not been merely between Yahweh and the human king of Egypt. It has been a spiritual power encounter too. Pharaoh claimed to be a god. Egypt had many gods. The plagues had already demonstrated Yahweh's superiority over some of them—as for example the attack on the Nile, the alleged divine source of Egypt's great fertility; or the darkening of the sun, the most powerful god of all in Egypt's pantheon. In this text, Yahweh makes it comprehensive. Whatever gods may be claimed in Egypt, Yahweh will act in judgment against them all.

Whatever gods and idols may actually be,[1] Yahweh the living God

---

[1]On the subject of gods and idols, whether they are "something" or "nothing," and what the Bible teaches in relation to them, see *The Mission of God* (Downers Grove, Ill.: InterVarsity Press, 2006), chap. 5.

will have none of them. They must fall before him, as much the target of his judgment as the fallen human beings who make them and worship them.

6. *That Yahweh is the protector of his people and victor over his enemies.*

But I will gain glory for myself through Pharaoh and all his army, and the Egyptians will know that I am the LORD. . . . The Egyptians will know that I am the LORD when I gain glory through Pharaoh, his chariots and his horsemen. (Ex 14:4, 18)

The learning spreads from Pharaoh alone to the whole nation of Egypt, who had been involved in the genocidal oppression. The climactic finale of the story unfolds in Exodus 14 with Pharaoh's army pursuing the fleeing Hebrews, who seem helplessly trapped between their enemy and the sea. But God has it under control (in fact Isaiah 43:16-17 interprets the events as Yahweh himself leading the Egyptian army to its own destruction). Even at this last moment, as had happened before (e.g., Ex 9:20; 11:3), those around Pharaoh recognize what he doggedly resisted right to the end—that the hand of Yahweh is in action. This time it is Pharaoh's own charioteers who know the truth of what is going on:

[Yahweh] made the wheels of their chariots come off so that they had difficulty driving [well, as you would!]. And the Egyptians said, "Let's get away from the Israelites! The LORD is fighting for them against Egypt." (Ex 14:25)

What a curriculum! This was a steep learning curve, which eventually ended in Pharaoh's own destruction. He certainly came to know God, but it did him no good in the end because he hardened his heart against the truth that was staring him in the face. Instead, he wriggled, rejected, resisted, repented, repented of his repentance, and in the end wrecked himself, his army and his country.[2] God is not mocked. Those who will not know him in submission to his authority will know him as the rock on which they stumble to destruction. Pharaoh chose this route and repeated his choice, against all appeals to change his mind—from Moses, from his own advisors, from God himself—until God accepted and reinforced the refusal he was determined to sustain.

Exodus 14 is the last word on that Pharaoh and his army. But we can be glad that it was not God's last word on Egypt in the Old Testament. For that we turn to Isaiah 19.

Isaiah 19 is a remarkable chapter, which begins by recording God's imminent judgment on the historical Egyptian empire of Isaiah's own day. But then, Isaiah 19:18-25 looks to the unspecified future and sees there a most breathtaking reversal of fortunes for Egypt. There is a deliberate reloading of the exodus narrative, with all the elements of deliverance and salvation now applied to the Egyptians themselves. The saving grace of God was never intended to be confined to the Israelites alone. Ultimately God's salvation turns even former enemies into his own people. It is well worth pausing to read Isaiah 19:18-25 to feel something of the amazement at this prophecy.

---

[2]The fact that the text says sometimes that God hardened Pharaoh's heart causes difficulty for some. It is important to note that while the whole narrative is certainly set within the outer framework of God's sovereignty, the prime responsibility for Pharaoh's stubborn resistance lies with Pharaoh himself. The dual fact of Pharaoh hardening his own heart and Yahweh hardening it, is referred to at the very beginning and end of the sequence (Ex. 7:3-4; 11:9-10). In between, we are told that Pharaoh hardened his heart eight times before we read of God's involvement again. In other words, the sequence is clearly Pharaoh's own stiffening resolve to reject the requests of Moses and the advice of his own counselors. Altogether we read that Pharaoh hardened his heart twelve times, whereas God is the subject six times, and five of these are towards the end of the story when Pharaoh's resistance has become irrevocable.

THE GOD ISRAEL CAME TO KNOW

Israel was not very far behind Pharaoh in their reluctance to know God, at the start of this narrative. That was one of the reasons Moses himself tried to opt out of the task of getting Israel out of Egypt. Would they believe him? Would they know the name of the God he was talking about? (Ex 3:13). And in the event, his fears were justified. No matter what God said or promised, the Israelites just didn't want to know, such was their cruel suffering (Ex 6:9).

On the other side of the Red Sea, things looked rather different, however. God's prediction that they would come to know him when he brought them out (Ex 6:6-8) had now been triumphantly fulfilled. They had witnessed not only his judgment on their enemies, but his amazing grace toward their plight.

Exodus 15 records the first reaction to this great event, a reaction of joyful praise and thanksgiving, celebrating not only the event itself, but also all that it proved about Yahweh. In fact, so much of Israel's knowledge of God is expressed in their songs of worship (as is true of us too, of course—which is why we need to be careful about the words we actually sing). What then, is particularly affirmed in this first song of Moses ("first," because there is another one in Deuteronomy 32)?

What was on the curriculum for Israel's knowing God at this stage of their journey with him?

That Yahweh is incomparable as God.

> Who among the gods is like you, O LORD?
>   Who is like you—
>   majestic in holiness,
>   awesome in glory,
>   working wonders? (Ex 15:11)

"Who is like you?" The question is rhetorical, of course. Moses is not asking for answers to be sent in with a list of candidates for comparison with Yahweh. The rhetorical question is actually a passionately strong affirmation: "There is *no god* that is anything like Yahweh at all!"

Yahweh had proved himself supreme over "all the gods of Egypt" (Ex 12:12), in the massive demonstration of power that constitutes the story of the plagues. Some people argue over whether this text (Ex 15:11) and others like it affirm "monotheism" in the strictest sense, but that is not really the focal point right here. All that matters is that Israel's God is clearly the most powerful God around. Yahweh is beyond comparison when it comes to a conflict of wills and power. Whoever or whatever the gods of Egypt may be (and Moses' song does not even trouble to name them, any more than he names the Pharaoh who claimed to be one of them), the God of Israel is more than a match for all of them.

The same kind of language is used elsewhere in the Old Testament to express wonder and admiration for Yahweh as the God without equal. When the Israelites said that "there is no God like Yahweh," they meant that no other god could ever compare with him. The God of Israel was beyond all comparison, for example,

- in keeping promises and fulfilling his word (2 Sam 7:22)
- in power and wisdom, especially as seen in creation (Jer 10:6-7, 11-12)
- in the heavenly assembly (Ps 89:6-8)
- in ruling over the nations (Jer 49:19; 50:44)
- in pardoning sin and forgiving transgression (Mic 7:18)
- in saving his people (Is 64:4)

And because there is no god like Yahweh, all nations will eventually come and worship *him* as the only true God (Ps 86:8-9; 96:4-9). This is the missional dimension of this great truth. Those who know the only true and living God must be committed to the vision of bringing all people to know him, too.

Of course, as we saw in chapter one, from Deuteronomy, this affirmation that there is no God like Yahweh quickly shades over into the stronger monotheistic affirmation that there is no other God at all. The reason why Yahweh is incomparable is because he actually *is* unique—he is utterly in a category of his own. There may be other things that human beings call gods and worship, but in reality they are not God—they do not have any divine being or substance. In fact, as the Old Testament repeatedly says, they are nothing more than the work of human hands. That too is something that "knowing God" means. It means knowing what is *not God,* and being able to distinguish between the two.

That Yahweh is sovereign as King.

The LORD will reign for ever and ever. (Ex 15:18)

This is the triumphant acclamation that comes at the climax of the song of Moses. It makes a very comprehensive claim. The form of the Hebrew verb has the flexibility of meaning "he has now demonstrated that he is king, he is now reigning, and he will go on reigning forever."

Now here we have the first significant time the kingdom of God is mentioned in the Bible, and it is important to notice the context. Yahweh is proclaimed as king because of his victory over those who have oppressed his people and refused to know him. So there is a confrontational dimension to this affirmation of Yahweh as king. Because *Yahweh* is king, all *other* kings (Egyptian or Canaanite) tremble, since they know what happened to the kings and gods of Egypt.

Israel, however, need not tremble but rejoice. For as a result of this great event, Israel now knows a great truth about their God,

Yahweh. And that truth is that the enemies of Yahweh (whether human or claimed deities), are no match for his victorious kingship. "The LORD is king," sings Moses, with the unspoken but clear implication, "*and not Pharaoh,* or any other of the claimed gods of Egypt or of Canaan."

The nature of Yahweh's kingship, however—that is, the way Yahweh actually functions as king—is unexpected. He exercises his kingship on behalf of the weak and oppressed. This is implied already in the song of Moses at the sea; what is being celebrated is precisely the liberation of an ethnic minority community who had been undergoing economic exploitation, political oppression and eventually a state-sponsored campaign of terrorizing genocide. But into the empire of Pharaoh steps the reign of Yahweh, the God who hears the cry of the oppressed, the God who hears, sees, remembers and is concerned (Ex 2:23-25).

Yahweh is incomparable as God and sovereign as king. These were the things Israel came to know as they watched in horrified awe the destruction of the enemy that had been crushing the life out of them. Here was the God to be reckoned with. Here was the God they needed to know in the dark years ahead of struggle in the land they were headed for. Sadly they all too quickly forgot, and ended up knowing God in the same way that the Egyptians did, i.e., through suffering his judgment. But that's another story.

The story of the exodus, then, shows us two groups of people who were exposed to God's judgment: Pharaoh and the Egyptians on the one hand, and the Israelites on the other. The former experienced it in action against themselves. The latter witnessed it in action on their behalf. In both cases, it was a profound experience of coming to know God in ways that neither side was quite prepared for when the whole exercise began.

CONCLUSION

What then, for us?

In chapter two, we stressed how knowing God includes knowing the stories in which God came to be known. So the first thing to say is that for us, knowing God must include knowing the things that Pharaoh and Israel came to know through this great demonstration of God in action. This is indeed the God we need to know in our own struggles. The Christian life involves the realities of suffering and persecution. It also involves spiritual warfare against our unseen enemy, the "roaring lion" who seeks to devour us, as Peter put it (1 Pet 5:8). And for many Christians in our world it involves endurance of the kind of hardship that is not unlike the experience of the Israelites in Egypt. We may not always expect deliverance on the spectacular scale of the exodus, but it is still the God of the exodus whom we are privileged to know. This is the God who rules in our land and throughout the earth; the God who will ultimately call to account all human authorities whom he has raised up for his own purpose. He is the God of Calvary and the empty tomb; the God above all gods; the God who reigns eternally but to whom we pray that his kingdom should come and his will be done on earth as in heaven. To know him is to cry out in praise,

"Who is a God like you?"

Who indeed?

4

4

Knowing God as the
Father of His People

Then say to Pharaoh, "This is what the LORD says: Israel is my
firstborn son, and I told you, 'Let my son go, so he may worship
me.' " (Ex 4:22-23)

I am Israel's father, and Ephraim is my firstborn son. (Jer 31:9)

You, O LORD, are our Father, our Redeemer from of old is your
name. (Is 63:16)

The Israelites may have been reluctant to address God routinely as
Father in worship (as the absence of such language from the book of
Psalms shows), but the concept of Yahweh as the father of his people
Israel was far from lacking in their theological repertoire, as the texts
above illustrate. We have already considered a possible reason for the
former reticence—namely the fact that Israel avoided the sexual
myths of other nations in which nations were birthed through the
sexual exploits of various gods and goddesses. Yahweh had not fathered Israel in any literal or polytheistic sense like that. Nevertheless, in reflecting on how God behaved toward them, Israel found it
natural to use the imagery of human parenthood as a way of describing the character and actions of God. God's protective, supportive,

compassionate and forgiving stance toward human beings could readily be portrayed by analogy with the best of human fathers. Yahweh God is fatherly, or father-like; and indeed, as we also saw at the end of the Introduction, motherly and mother-like too.

In this chapter, however, we go beyond those parental portraits to more direct texts that affirm a relationship of sonship and fatherhood between Israel and God. In many ways this is simply another way of speaking about the covenant relationship, but we shall notice ways in which it extends even beyond that.

The Old Testament speaks of *Israel* (and Israel's king) as Yahweh's son. Inevitably, therefore, this forms a rich and profound context within which *Jesus* considered himself to be the Son of God. Certainly Jesus' own consciousness of God as his Father, and the rest of the New Testament's portrayal of his divine sonship, has deep roots in this Old Testament affirmation of the filial dimension of Israel's relationship to Yahweh. I have explored all this much more fully in *Knowing Jesus Through the Old Testament*.[1] So in this chapter we shall concentrate primarily on the Old Testament understanding of this dynamic relationship, but it is impossible as a Christian to do so for long without recognizing where and to whom the trajectories of fatherhood and sonship eventually lead. That was a major motivation in writing the other book.

GOD AS FATHER AND ISRAEL AS SON

When we assemble and analyze all the texts in the Old Testament that speak about Yahweh as father of Israel, or Israel as the son (or the sons) of Yahweh, we can detect two main ways in which the terms are

---

[1]Christopher J. H. Wright, *Knowing Jesus Through the Old Testament* (Downers Grove, Ill.: InterVarsity Press, 1992; Oxford: Monarch, 2005), chap. 3, "Jesus and His Old Testament Identity."

used.[2] On the one hand there are texts which use the singular "son" as a description of Israel collectively as a nation. These are mostly positive affirmations about Israel's status before God. On the other hand there are texts which use the plural "sons" (often translated as "children" in the NIV) as a description of the Israelites. These are mostly negative comments on how the Israelites were behaving in anything but the way that sons ought to behave. But then beyond these two categories, we find a third—namely that if God is Israel's Father then there can be grounds for hope even beyond a broken covenant and inevitable judgment. So we turn to these three aspects of our theme.

A given status. The concept of Yahweh as father and Israel as son goes back very early. The song of Moses in Deuteronomy 32 is reckoned by most scholars to be among the earliest poetic texts in the Bible, and it clearly uses this concept. Indeed, it applies the combined parental roles of both father and mother to God.

> Is he not your Father, your Creator,
> who made you and formed you? (Deut 32:6)

> You deserted the Rock, who fathered you;
> you forgot the God who gave you birth. (Deut 32:18)

And in the narrative historical texts, the assertion that Israel is Yahweh's firstborn son comes even before the exodus, and as part of the justification for it (Ex 4:22-23—quoted above). This is a tradition that Hosea clearly knew and quoted. The exodus involved God bringing his own son out of Egypt:

> When Israel was a child, I loved him,
> and out of Egypt I called my son. (Hos 11:1)

---

[2]It would be worth pausing to scan through the list which includes: Ex. 4:22; Deut. 14:1; 32:6, 18-19; Isa. 1:2; 30:1, 9; 43:6; 63:16; 64:8; Jer. 3:4, 19; 4:22; 31:9, 20; Hos. 11:1; Mal. 1:6; 2:10.

In these verses, "you" and "son" are in the singular. The whole nation is in view a single entity. This is true also in Jeremiah 31.

> I am Israel's father,
> and Ephraim is my firstborn son. (Jer 31:9)

> Is not Ephraim my dear son,
> The child in whom I delight? (Jer 31:20)

The point here is that Israel as a whole nation owed its existence to Yahweh. He is the God who had created them and called them onto the stage of history. The metaphor of sonship, in this respect, is another way of picturing the theological affirmation of Israel's election—i.e., that God had chosen Israel to be his people for the sake of bringing blessing to the nations. But it takes it back a step further by suggesting that it was not the case that Israel was an already existing nation whom God then subsequently decided to choose and use. Rather, Israel was brought into existence for this chosen purpose. This was what they were born for. Their creation, election and calling were "simultaneous" realities—theologically, even if the story from the call of Abraham to the existence of the redeemed people of Israel after the exodus took several centuries.

Furthermore, the metaphor of sonship excludes any merits or conditions. You don't choose to be born or deserve to be born. You just are. You exist because your parents chose to conceive and birth you. The choice was theirs not yours. In that sense, sonship is an objective *given* status, independent of what you may think of it or how you respond to it. In the same way,

> What is clear is that it was not by Israel's choice or action that they are Yahweh's son, nor does the status and privilege involved derive in any sense from Israel's own action or merits. In this re-

spect, Israel's sonship is a *given* which corresponds entirely with the unconditional, indicative *given* of their election. Israel is the firstborn son of Yahweh for no other reason than that Yahweh brought them as a nation into existence, just as they are the people of Yahweh for no other reason than that he "set his love upon" them and chose them for himself (Deut 7:6-7).[3]

Grounds for rebuke. When the language of sonship is used in the plural it is mostly (though not exclusively) in a negative context of accusation. The Israelites are addressed as sons of Yahweh, but then rebuked for failing to fulfill the normal expectations of sons to fathers—namely respect and obedience, within a relationship of trust and gratitude. So, whereas the use of "son" in the singular tends to express the indicative reality of Israel's status before God, the use of "sons" in the plural tends to express the imperative expectation of obedience.

The first use of the plural in Deuteronomy sets the expectation. If Israel as a whole people is holy, then all individual Israelites, as sons, must manifest that practical holiness before him.

Sons, that is what you [plural] are, belonging to Yahweh your God. So do not cut yourselves or shave the front of your heads for the dead. For a holy people, that is what you [singular] are, belonging to Yahweh your God. You [singular] are the one Yahweh chose to be his people, his treasured possession out of all the peoples that are on the face of the earth. (Deut 14:1-2, author's translation)

Such expectations were repeatedly dashed, however, by the his-

---

[3]Christopher J. H. Wright, *God's People in God's Land: Family, Land and Property in the Old Testament* (Grand Rapids: Eerdmans; Carlisle: Paternoster, 1990), pp. 17-18.

tory of Israel in the land, so much so that prophets use the picture of sonship not as an assurance but as an accusation. What kind of way was this for sons to behave? Even earthly fathers received better treatment from their sons than Yahweh was getting from his Israelite sons.

1. They were rebellious and corrupt.

Hear, O heavens! Listen, O earth!
>For the LORD has spoken:
>"I reared children [sons] and brought them up,
>but they have rebelled against me.
The ox knows his master,
>the donkey his owner's manger,
>but Israel does not know,
>my people do not understand."
Ah, sinful nation,
>a people loaded with guilt,
>a brood of evildoers,
>children [sons] given to corruption!
>They have forsaken the LORD;
>they have spurned the Holy One of Israel
>and turned their backs on him. (Is 1:2-4)

2. They were faithless and hypocritically treacherous. In spite of all God's desire to show generous parental affection, and in spite of all their rhetorical appeals to his paternal indulgence:

Have you not just called to me:
>"My Father, my friend from my youth,
will you always be angry?
>Will your wrath continue forever?"
>This is how you talk,

but you do all the evil you can. . . .
I myself said,
  "How gladly would I treat you like sons
  and give you a desirable land,
  the most beautiful inheritance of any nation."
  I thought you would call me "Father"
  and not turn away from following me.
But like a woman unfaithful to her husband,
  so you have been unfaithful to me, O house of Israel,
  declares the LORD. (Jer 3:4-5, 19-20)

3. They were obstinate, contrary, deceitful and incorrigible.

"Woe to the obstinate children [sons],"
  declares the LORD,
  "to those who carry out plans that are not mine,
  forming an alliance, but not by my Spirit,
  heaping sin upon sin." . . .
These are rebellious people, deceitful children [sons],
  children unwilling to listen to the LORD's instruction.
(Is 30:1, 9)

Not surprisingly, even at the end of the Old Testament period, God was still lamenting the lack of honor and respect that he, Israel's father, was receiving from such feckless progeny.

"A son honors his father, and a servant his master. If I am a father, where is the honor due me? If I am a master, where is the respect due me?" says the LORD Almighty. (Mal 1:6)

So as we put both of the above sections together, we can clearly discern the same duality that is inherent in the covenant relationship.

That is to say, the balance and tension between the unconditional givenness of the relationship on the one hand (Israel had done nothing to initiate or deserve it), and the imperative dimension of the response expected from Israel, on the other hand (the response of love, trust and obedience). The father-son relationship embodies the same dynamic tension.

This understanding of the relationship between Yahweh and Israel provided a rich source for the New Testament's understanding of the relationship between God the Father and those who are believers in his Son Jesus Christ. For there too, on the one hand, we are brought into a relationship of adoption and election, by God's unconditional and unmerited grace, while on the other hand we are called into a life of responsive and trusting obedience, as befits the children of our heavenly Father.

Grounds for hope. We have drawn parallels between the language of sonship and the covenant. And in the broad sweep of biblical teaching that is correct. To know God as Father through becoming a child of God through faith in his Son is the same thing as being brought into the new covenant relationship with God through the blood of Christ, and is equally eternal. However, in the specific context of the Old Testament, the two can be distinguished somewhat, inasmuch as the relationship of son to father has an enduring permanence that survived even the broken Sinai covenant. You can break a covenant, but you can't stop being a son of your father. Likewise, though Israel knew the shattering reality of a broken covenant as they languished in exile, they could still turn to God in hope. After all, God's assertion that Israel was his firstborn son had been made even before the exodus, before Sinai (Ex 4:22). And it was still there even amid the wreckage of that covenant. Thus, Jeremiah, who could anticipate the profound and permanent joy of a new covenant, finds a more emotional foundation for hope in God's inability, as father, to cast off his errant son forever. The One who brought his firstborn out of Egypt would bring the same son back from exile.

> They will come with weeping;
>> they will pray as I bring them back.
> I will lead them beside streams of water
> on a level path where they will not stumble,
> because I am Israel's father,
> and Ephraim is my firstborn son.
> "Hear the word of the LORD, O nations;
>> proclaim it in distant coastlands:
>> 'He who scattered Israel will gather them
>> and will watch over his flock like a shepherd.' "
> (Jer 31:9-10)

> "Is not Ephraim my dear son,
>> the child in whom I delight?
> Though I often speak against him,
> I still remember him.
> Therefore my heart yearns for him;
> I have great compassion for him,"
> declares the LORD. (Jer 31:20)

Isaiah celebrates the same hope for God's children. Those who are the sons and daughters of the living God cannot languish forever in exile.

> I will say to the north, "Give them up!"
>> and to the south, "Do not hold them back."
> Bring my sons from afar
> and my daughters from the ends of the earth—
> everyone who is called by my name,

whom I created for my glory,
whom I formed and made. (Is 43:6-7)

And in the time of waiting and longing, the people of Israel themselves knew that, while lamenting their own covenant-breaking unfaithfulness, they could still appeal to the father heart of God for restorative compassion and mercy. The fatherhood of God provided grounds for hope for a contrite people.

Look down from heaven and see
    from your lofty throne, holy and glorious.
    Where are your zeal and your might?
    Your tenderness and compassion are withheld from us.
But you are our Father,
    though Abraham does not know us
    or Israel acknowledge us;
    you, O LORD, are our Father,
    our Redeemer from of old is your name.
(Is 63:15-16, italics added)

No one calls on your name
    or strives to lay hold of you;
    for you have hidden your face from us
    and made us waste away because of our sins.
Yet, O LORD, you are our Father.
    We are the clay, you are the potter;
    we are all the work of your hand.
Do not be angry beyond measure, O LORD;
    do not remember our sins forever.
    Oh, look upon us, we pray,
    For we are all your people. (Is 64:7-9)

In *Knowing Jesus Through the Old Testament* I suggested that this dimension of assured permanence in the relationship of son to father in Old Testament Israel's relationship with God was one of the factors that nourished the confidence of Jesus in his own guaranteed future. Why did Jesus repeatedly affirm the certainty of his own resurrection? How could he be so sure? Because he knew his identity and his Scriptures. His identity as the Son of God meant that he was the messianic embodiment of Israel, God's son. And from the Scriptures he knew that God had always remained faithful to his firstborn son, Israel—even in their unfaithfulness to him; how much more would he preserve and vindicate his faithful, obedient and sinless Son?[4]

But we can go further than the way the Old Testament concept of God's fatherhood strengthened *Jesus* as God's Son. For clearly it also underpins *our* eternal security in Christ, as Paul so richly taught. We cannot expound here all the texts in the New Testament concerning what it means to be children of God, knowing him as Father with the same intimacy that Jesus called on him as *Abba*. A glimpse at Romans 8 will have to suffice. Sonship and security are gloriously intertwined in this climax to Paul's argument in the first part of his letter.

First of all we need to remind ourselves of Paul's central point in the previous chapters of Romans. Jews and Gentiles stand on the same footing before God in regard to sin, and equally they stand on the same footing in regard to salvation. For Jew and Gentile alike, the only way into right relationship with God and membership of his redeemed and covenant people, is through the Messiah, Jesus. But that one way is open to all—Jew or Gentile. Therefore the promises of God to Israel are now available, through Christ and the gospel, to people of all nations. The privilege of being sons of God is no longer

---

[4]*Knowing Jesus*, pp. 125-28.

confined to one ethnic group—the Jews; rather, people of any nation can enjoy that status in Christ and effectively become part of the expanded Israel of God. To be in Christ is to be in Abraham. And to be in Christ is to share in the sonship that God's Spirit grants us. And to share in that sonship means to have an inheritance that is eternal and glorious.

> For you did not receive a spirit that makes you a slave again to fear, but you received the Spirit of sonship. And by him we cry, "*Abba*, Father." The Spirit himself testifies with our spirit that we are God's children. Now if we are children, then we are heirs—heirs of God and co-heirs with Christ, if indeed we share in his sufferings in order that we may also share in his glory. (Rom 8:15-17)

From that foundation, Paul goes on to draw breathtaking cosmic implications—for the whole creation also looks forward to what our redeemed sonship will eventually entail, even if it groans along with us and the Holy Spirit in the meantime.

> The creation waits in eager expectation for the sons of God to be revealed. For the creation was subjected to frustration, not by its own choice, but by the will of the one who subjected it, in hope that the creation itself will be liberated from its bondage to decay and brought into the glorious freedom of the children of God. (Rom 8:19-21)

And if the will of the Creator is our ultimate glorification in the likeness of his own Son (Rom 8:28-30), and if the whole of creation is the object his redemptive purpose, then there is nobody and nothing "in all creation" that can threaten our eternal security as the children of God (Rom 8:31-39).

For I am convinced that neither death nor life, neither angels
nor demons, neither the present nor the future, nor any pow-
ers, neither height nor depth, nor anything else in all creation,
will be able to separate us from the love of God that is in Christ
Jesus our Lord. (Rom 8:38-39)

In this wonderful passage, Paul has transformed and expanded the
faith of Israel, which of course was in his bloodstream and the very
foundation of his whole worldview. Israel knew what it was to call
God Father and to turn to him as sons. It was a relationship that was
founded on the gracious initiative of God's election. And it was a relationship that had demanded of them an obedience they so often
failed to deliver. But in Jesus of Nazareth, Israel's Messiah, that relationship had been seen in its perfection. Now it was available in
Christ to people of any and every nation, just as God had promised
Abraham. And so, for us, as in so many other ways, what we have in
Christ is not a denial or rejection of the faith of Old Testament Israel,
but rather its enriched and expanded fulfillment and the eternal security of what it had pointed toward in Christ.

GOD AS FATHER OF ISRAEL'S KING

Having focused briefly on Christ for a moment, we are drawn back
to another dimension of the father-son relationship in the Old Testament which undoubtedly also impacted Jesus' sense of identity and
mission. That is, the way God addressed not just Israel in general, but
Israelite kings in particular, as "my son."

The historical kings. In the ancient world human rulers and
judges could commonly be called "sons of God" (or the son of a particular god). This did not necessarily mean they were regarded as
gods, or divine incarnations—though certainly some did claim that

for themselves. It was simply a way of saying that their authority derived from God (or the national god) and that in some way, their decisions and actions reflected what God (or the gods in polytheistic contexts) wanted to accomplish. Thus, for example, in Psalm 82, the target of God's anger is actually human judges who were failing to deliver justice as God demanded it. But God says to them, contrasting the high calling he had given them with their actual practice and dismal destiny,

> I said, "You are 'gods';
>> you are all sons of the Most High."
> But you will die like mere men;
>> you will fall like every other ruler. (Ps 82:6-7)

So it is not unusual that when God made his very specific covenant promise to David and his household after him, that he and his sons would reign over Israel forever, he used the language of sonship to frame the relationship that David and his successors would have with God. God would be father to the king, just as he was ultimately father to the people.

However, what is more unusual is the strong emphasis in the Old Testament texts on the requirement of *obedience* that this royal sonship involved. Israel's king, as a son of Yahweh, was subject to the same filial discipline as the rest of the Israelites. He was certainly not above punishment. And so we find, even in the inaugural promise to David, the same combination of unconditional promise ("forever"), and necessary ethical sanctions (punishment for wrongdoing), that we saw in the case of Israel's status and responsibilities as son (or sons) of God. Here is how God put it to David:

> When your days are over and you rest with your fathers, I will

raise up your offspring to succeed you, who will come from your own body, and I will establish his kingdom. He is the one who will build a house for my Name, and I will establish the throne of his kingdom forever. *I will be his father, and he will be my son.* When he does wrong, I will punish him with the rod of men, with floggings inflicted by men. But my love will never be taken away from him, as I took it away from Saul, whom I removed from before you. Your house and your kingdom will endure forever before me; your throne will be established forever. (2 Sam 7:12-16, italics added)

Even before David, when Samuel had (with considerable reluctance) appointed Saul as Israel's first king, he made it very clear that the standards of obedience God required from Israel as a nation applied just as much to their king. The king was not above the law.

Now here is the king you have chosen, the one you asked for; see, the LORD has set a king over you. If you fear the LORD and serve and obey him and do not rebel against his commands, and if *both you and the king* who reigns over you follow the LORD your God—good! But if you do not obey the LORD, and if you rebel against his commands, his hand will be against you, as it was against your fathers. . . . Yet if you persist in doing evil, *both you and your king* will be swept away. (1 Sam 12:13-15, 25, italics added)

This was entirely consistent with the law in Deuteronomy that had permitted Israel to appoint a king, if they chose to do so. Along with various criteria for selection there is a clear instruction to faithful covenant obedience, demonstrated in knowing and practicing God's law.

When he takes the throne of his kingdom, he is to write for

himself on a scroll a copy of this law, taken from that of the priests, who are Levites. It is to be with him, and he is to read it all the days of his life so that he may learn to revere the LORD his God and follow carefully all the words of this law and these decrees and not consider himself better than his brothers and turn from the law to the right or to the left. Then he and his descendants will reign a long time over his kingdom in Israel. (Deut 17:18-20)

In other words, Israel's king was not to be a *super-Israelite*, lording it over his subjects, but a *model Israelite*, setting them an example of what it meant to be an obedient son of Yahweh.

If only . . .

The fact is that almost every historical king, both in the line of David and in the separated northern kingdom of Israel after Solomon, failed to be such a model. God's sons, the kings, failed in their duty of obedience just as much as God's son, the nation of Israel did in theirs. In fact the nation's moral state usually reflected the monarch's lead—for good or ill.

What then would become of the promise God had made to the sons of David? This is where the historical tradition of frustrated expectations flows over into the eschatological tradition of messianic hope. There would come such a king, great David's greater son, the royal Son himself.

The messianic king. In some of the psalms we find affirmation of the king as a son of God. The most well known comes right near the beginning of the book of Psalms—in a pair of psalms that were probably quite deliberately put side by side here as a key note for the whole book.

Psalm 1 holds up a picture of the model Israelite—walking in the way of the LORD, studying and obeying his law, avoiding the paths of wickedness. It is a plausible suggestion that the opening psalm is intentionally a portrait not only of the model Israelite, but also of the model king—who should have been living like this, according to Deuteronomy 17. But we also know, from Deuteronomy 4:6-8, that if Israel were to live in faithful obedience to God's law, this would make them a visible model to other nations, who would be drawn to the quality of spiritual and ethical life demonstrated in Israel.[5]

Psalm 2, however, portrays the nations, far from submitting in willing obedience to Yahweh, in continuing rebellion against him and his anointed king. The psalm begins with the fundamental question "Why?"—which is not explicitly answered in the psalm itself. One suggested answer is that the historical kings of Israel have so radically failed to live in the light of Psalm 1 that Israel itself has joined the ranks of the rebels. There would then be a tension between the "coronation" words of Psalm 2:7 and the historical reality of persistently disobedient kings. All the kings in the line of David would have heard the words:

> I will proclaim the decree of the LORD:
>   He said to me, "You are my Son;
>   today I have become your Father. (Ps 2:7)

And all of them would have known the ethical content of the prayer for the king in Psalm 72:

> Endow the king with your justice, O God,
>   the *royal son* with your righteousness.
> He will judge your people in righteousness,
>   your afflicted ones with justice. (Ps 72:1-2, italics added)

---

[5]I owe this thought and the suggestion in the following paragraphs to the conversations with John Wigfield during his doctoral research.

Psalm 72 goes on to spell out the expectations of the king—care for the poor and needy, purging oppression, compassion for the weak, rescue from bloodshed and violence. But the fact is that the reigns of almost all the kings turned these things upside down, neglecting the weak and contributing to a steady escalation of injustice, bloodshed and oppression. So how can Psalm 72 be read except either as an idealized hope, or as a hollow critique of the present?

So Psalm 89 cries out with the starkest possible tension between the original hope and the actual reality. There is a screaming contradiction. The psalm first celebrates the original promise to David, including the status and responsibilities of sonship:

> He will call out to me, "You are my Father,
>   my God, the Rock my Savior."
> I will also appoint him my firstborn,
>   the most exalted of the kings of the earth.
>   I will maintain my love to him forever,
>   and my covenant with him will never fail.
> I will establish his line forever,
>   his throne as long as the heavens endure.
>
> "If his sons forsake my law
>   and do not follow my statutes,
> if they violate my decrees
>   and fail to keep my commands,
> I will punish their sin with the rod,
>   their iniquity with flogging;
> but I will not take my love from him,
>   nor will I ever betray my faithfulness.
> I will not violate my covenant

or alter what my lips have uttered.
Once for all, I have sworn by my holiness—
    and I will not lie to David—
that his line will continue forever
    and his throne endure before me like the sun;
it will be established forever like the moon,
    the faithful witness in the sky." (Ps 89:26-37)

But then the psalm goes on abruptly to acknowledge the historical abyss into which all this seemed to have fallen, with the collapse of the kingdom of Judah, the destruction of Jerusalem, the exile of the people, and the end of David's royal line (at least in terms of reigning kings).

But you [God] have rejected, you have spurned,
    you have been very angry with your anointed one.
You have renounced the covenant with your servant
    and have defiled his crown in the dust. (Ps 89:38-39)

But had he?

Who, exactly, had rejected and spurned whom? Was it not the repeated and incorrigible wickedness of Israel's kings and people that had led to the fracture of the covenant and the punishment of exile? Indeed so. But what then could become of the promises to David? Who then would reign on his throne forever?

There is no doubt that psalms like Psalm 2, 72 and 89 were already being interpreted messianically even within Old Testament times, and certainly by the time of the New Testament. That is to say, they were understood not only as having originally applied to David and the historical kings that followed him, but also as having a prophetic dimension. They pointed forward to One who would come, as a son of David and (like David but more so) as the Son of God; One who would fulfill the expectations of reigning in justice, fruitfulness and peace, not only over Israel but over the nations.

And these, of course, were precisely the expectations that the New Testament affirms were realized in Jesus of Nazareth, though their complete fulfillment lies ahead of us in our expectation of his return to reign in glory. The identity of Jesus as the messianic son of David, the royal Son of God, was affirmed to him in the words of his Father at his baptism, clearly echoing Psalm 2:7: "You are my Son, whom I love; with you I am well pleased" (Mk 1:11).[6]

Many of the prophets pointed forward in a similar way, using different figures and pictures to express this hope, including the coming of a true son of David. But one mysterious, though extremely well-known, prophetic text combines sonship and fatherhood in a tantalizing way.

Among all Isaiah's great prophetic visions of the messianic era to come, perhaps the most well known (through its repeated reading at Christmas) is Isaiah 9:1-7. The future era that will bring light, hope, joy, justice and peace will be inaugurated through the gift of a son—a gift of God himself, of course, as the passive verb ("is given") implies.

> For to us a child is born,
>> to us *a son* is given,
>> and the government will be on his shoulders.
> And he will be called
>> Wonderful Counselor, Mighty God,
>> *Everlasting Father,* Prince of Peace.

---

[6]The words of the Father at Jesus' baptism probably also echo Isaiah 42:1 and Genesis 22:2. For further reflection on these connections, see *Knowing Jesus Through the Old Testament,* chap. 3.

> Of the increase of his government and peace
>   there will be no end.
> He will reign on David's throne
>   and over his kingdom,
> establishing and upholding it
>   with justice and righteousness
>   from that time on and forever.
> The zeal of the LORD Almighty
>   will accomplish this. (Is 9:6-7, italics added)

The most remarkable and mysterious phrase in this wonderful text is the third of the four titles given to this divine son: "Everlasting Father." What can it mean for one who is a son to be named as father? In terms of Old Testament concepts, it must refer to the governance dimension of his role. Fathers were expected to rule their households. God as Father was the true Lord and King of his people, exercising his government (or seeking to) through human kings. This given Son, then, will be the one on whose shoulders the government of the Father will rest. The rule of this coming one will reflect the fatherly qualities of God himself. So he can even be given that name and title with astonishing boldness—a boldness matched only by the preceding title—"Mighty God."

Christians will see what God did in Jesus as guaranteeing the vision's fulfilment. In Jesus we see the evidence that the Mighty God really will bring to effect a wonderful purpose and that the Everlasting Father will act effectively as a commander, for the sake of the people's spiritual and physical well-being. . . . The passage is a vision of what God is committed to achieving through David's line. It receives partial fulfilment in the achievements of kings such as Hezekiah and Josiah, and then a fulfilment in Jesus that is potentially final even if its potentiality remains unrealized. It thus still indicates the agenda to which God has made a commitment and gives human beings grounds for hope.[7]

In New Testament fulfillment, it is reflected in the unity of Father and Son, so profoundly articulated by Jesus himself on various occasions. His will was to do his Father's will. "I and the Father are one" (Jn 10:30). And it is further reflected in the apostolic teaching that the rule of the Messiah is effectively the rule of the Father—now and for all eternity. To know God the Son is to know God the Father. The lordship of Christ and the sovereignty of God the Father are one. And to submit in loving obedience to God's Son is to do the will of the Father.

CONCLUSION

What, then, have we learned in this chapter about knowing God the Father through the Old Testament?

Possibly the most significant contribution this chapter will have made to our understanding will be as a counterbalance to our tendency to think of the fatherhood of God in primarily personal and spiritual terms. Now of course it is entirely proper to enjoy a personal relationship with God as Father. This was modeled, promised and taught by Jesus himself; it is the gift and witness of the Holy Spirit in our hearts; it is the birthright of every child of God. We thank God profoundly for this intimate relationship and for his fatherly love, provision, guidance and protection. And as we shall see in the next chapter, such intimacy with God was not at all foreign to the faith of Old Testament Israel.

However, we need to expand our horizons beyond our personal

---

[7]John Goldingay, *Isaiah,* New International Biblical Commentary (Peabody, Mass.: Hendrickson; Carlisle: Paternoster, 2001), p. 72.

enjoyment of God's fatherhood and build into our Christian thinking those dimensions of it that we have explored here. For we have seen that the primary way the Old Testament speaks of God as Father is corporate—that is, as Father of his people Israel. This powerful metaphor for the collective relationship between God and his people connects several key truths.

It speaks of the given status and security that we enjoy by belonging to this people. God has chosen to make us part of the people whom he has "brought to birth" and of whom he rejoices to be called Father. That is why, for example, the Lord's Prayer begins, *"Our* Father."

But it also speaks of the responsibility that rests upon us as children of our Father. As we saw, the prime duty of Israel toward God, as son to father, was that of obedience within the covenant. The use of the parental metaphor preserves the relational dimension. Obedience in the Old Testament was never intended to be (as it is often caricatured), a blind or slavish adherence to impersonal external regulations. The warmth and profoundly personal language of psalms like 19 and 119 rule out that kind of misconception. Rather, the whole relationship between God's people and God as Father should indeed be one of authority on the one hand and obedience on the other, but set within a framework of love, provision, security and trust.

And finally, we have noted that the father-son imagery was used in relation to Israel's kings, in such a way that it eventually flows over into the messianic kingship of Jesus, the true Son of God. This means that we must always include within our understanding of God as Father the reality of his governance of history, his rule over the nations, exercised in and through his Son, our Lord Jesus Christ. That is also why the Lord's Prayer, addressed to "Our Father," begins with the prayer that his sovereign will be done on earth and ends with the acknowledgment of his kingdom, power and glory.

5

Knowing God Through Engaging Him in Prayer

It may have come as some surprise that the theme of knowing God, in earlier chapters, has largely been a matter of corporate or national knowing. Whether through the collective experience of God's redeeming grace, or through being the objects or witnesses of God's judgment, Israel and Egypt as whole nations came to know Yahweh as God in ways they had not done before. We can't dismiss or diminish such examples of our theme, since the language of knowing God is used repeatedly by the Bible itself in these contexts, as we have seen. Nevertheless, we may be wondering, surely "knowing God" is a personal and intimate matter, more to do with the devotional life of prayer and spiritual engagement with God. Is there nothing of that dimension of knowing God in the Old Testament? There is, of course, and we would immediately think of the close relationship between God and Joseph, Hannah, Samuel, David, many anonymous psalmists, Jeremiah, Nehemiah, Daniel and others.

In this chapter we shall consider the two most outstanding examples of a personal relationship of knowing God in the Old Testament—Abraham and Moses. Particularly we shall focus on an incident of intercessory prayer in the life of each, and see what it has to tell us about the way they knew God. Both are described as men whom *God* claimed to "know," though the text itself is more explicit about Moses specifically wanting to know God than in Abraham's case, where it is more inferential, but equally clear. In both cases they have an enormous amount to teach us about what it means to know the living God and engage with him in the meaningful, personal and challenging dialogue of prayer.

ABRAHAM—GOD'S FRIEND

Three times in the Bible, Abraham is described as "God's friend" (2 Chron 20:7; Is 41:8; Jas 2:23). The word literally means "loved one." When we read the story of Genesis 18, it is not hard to see why. Jesus once said that a man may not tell his servants what he is doing, but he will share his plans with his friends (Jn 15:14-15). His Father had taken the same stance with Abraham, feeling almost obliged to share his plans with him—a sign of intimate friendship (Gen 18:17). So let's look at the story and detect the marks of this divine-human intimacy. It is a story that takes two chapters, beginning at Genesis 18:1 and concluding at Genesis 19:29, yet it covers less than 24 hours in the life of Abraham—from one afternoon to the next daybreak. But what a day!

Abraham's intimacy with God.

The LORD appeared to Abraham near the great trees of Mamre while he was sitting at the entrance to his tent in the heat of the day. Abraham looked up and saw three men standing nearby. When he saw them, he hurried from the entrance of his tent to meet them and bowed low to the ground.

He said, "If I have found favor in your eyes, my lord, do not pass your servant by. Let a little water be brought, and then you may all wash your feet and rest under this tree. Let me get you something to eat, so you can be refreshed and then go on your way—now that you have come to your servant."

"Very well," they answered, "do as you say."

So Abraham hurried into the tent to Sarah. "Quick," he said, "get three seahs of fine flour and knead it and bake some bread." Then he ran to the herd and selected a choice, tender calf and gave it to a servant, who hurried to prepare it. He then brought some curds and milk and the calf that had been prepared, and set these before them. While they ate, he stood near them under a tree. (Gen 18:1-8)

The story is exquisitely and expertly told. The narrator tells the reader in Genesis 18:1 that Yahweh appeared to Abraham, but of course Abraham did not know this at first. So we have the gentle irony that we know more than the main character in the story knows—initially at least. This is similar to the beginning of Genesis 22, where the reader is told that the story to follow involved Yahweh testing Abraham—but Abraham does not know that it is only a test. God and the reader know that God will not go through with what he tells Abraham to do—but Abraham did not. For if he had, it would not have been the test that it was. Similarly here, we watch as Abraham responds with customary but abnormally generous hospitality to three strangers who have unexpectedly disturbed his siesta. Part of the irony is that Abraham demonstrates his knowledge of God in behaving this way even when he does not actually know it is God he is entertaining—a point not lost as an incentive to hospitality by Hebrews 13:2.

However, as the story proceeds, there are hints as to who at least one of these mysterious visitors must be, even though it is hard to say exactly when the penny dropped for Abraham. The fact that recognition of the Lord takes place in the course of a meal echoes a similar moment of recognition one Sunday evening in a home in Emmaus.

But what is happening here? God himself has come to dinner! As Kent Hughes points out,[1] this is the only occasion in the whole Bible, prior to the incarnation of God in Christ, where God eats with a human being. On other occasions when people made a meal for an angel of the Lord, it was consumed in flames as a burnt offering (Judg 6:18-24; 13:15-21). At the time of the making of the covenant at Mount Sinai, the elders of Israel went up the mountain with Moses and Aaron and his sons, where they had a vision of God, and then ate and drank without harm (Ex 24:9-11). On that occasion, the elders ate in the presence of God. But here, God eats in the presence of Abraham, standing attentively nearby in the shade of the tree. This is a moment of rare, indeed unique, intimacy.

When the meal was over, we read later "Abraham walked along with them to see them on their way" (Gen 18:16). Abraham, who eats with God, now walks with God (as Enoch had done), and in a moment also talks with God. A friend indeed. Actually, "to see them on their way" is literally "to send them." Abraham, who years before had obeyed God's sending, is now the one sending God on his way! This storyteller has a fine eye for small ironies—but they all paint a picture of an intimate relationship.

The purpose of knowing, and being known by, God. The friendship had not started from Abraham's side, however. As we know from the narrative since Genesis 12, it was God who took the initiative in calling Abraham out of his homeland in Mesopotamia, with the twin

---

[1]P. Kent Hughes, *Genesis: Beginning and Blessing* (Wheaton, Ill.: Crossway Books, 2004), pp. 254-55.

command, "Go . . . and . . . be a blessing" (Gen 12:1-3), and a suite of promises to accompany him. Abraham's response of obedience and trust had sealed the beginning of the relationship and characterized it ever more deeply, coming to a searing and soaring climax in Genesis 22.

At this point, then, it is God who recalls the relational truth that if Abraham has now come to know God it is because God first knew him. By this point in the story, readers are sure that both Abraham and Sarah have tumbled (embarrassingly, in Sarah's case) to the realization that one of these three hearty appetites belongs to none other than God (for reasons we shall see in a moment). But as the meal breaks up and the guests are about to resume their journey, God himself chooses to reveal more than just his true identity and to disclose his intentions also.

> Then the LORD said, "Shall I hide from Abraham what I am about to do? Abraham will surely become a great and powerful nation, and all nations on earth will be blessed through him. For I have *known* him, *in order that* he will instruct his children and his household after him to keep the way of the LORD by doing righteousness and justice, *in order that* the LORD will bring about for Abraham what he has promised him." (Gen 18:17-19, author's translation and italics)

"I have known him," says God. This is usually and rightly translated, "I have chosen him," since that is exactly the meaning of God's knowledge in this case (as likewise of Israel as a whole, in Amos 3:2, where the same word is used). But it still important to feel the full flavor of the actual word in Hebrew. The intimate relationship between Abraham and God is, first and foremost, because God knows Abraham, not the other way around.

The point however is not merely chronological—who knew whom first. The point is profoundly purposeful. If Abraham has come to know God, it is because God knew him *for a purpose*. In fact it was for a double purpose, which is clear from the repeated and emphatic "in order that" in verse 19. The nearer purpose (in the middle of the verse) relates to the kind of community Abraham was to cultivate by his teaching. The longer term purpose (in the final clause of the verse) relates to God's promise that through Abraham he would bless all nations on earth. These double purposes clearly mirror the dual content of the original promise that Abraham would himself become a great nation under God's blessing, and that all nations would be blessed through him.

1. *Blessing.* Taking the longer vision first: God's choice of Abraham was for the purpose of blessing the nations. That was God's mission, God's long-term redemptive goal, and the launch pad of the whole of the rest of the Bible's story.[2] If Abraham had not got up and left his homeland in obedience to God, the Bible would have been a very thin book indeed. But because he did, the whole grand narrative of the Bible ran its course, and runs it still, for its climactic ending yet lies ahead of us. And that ending will see people from every tribe and language and people and nations, in fulfillment of God's promise to Abraham, gathered before the throne of God as his redeemed humanity in the new creation (Rev 7:9).

So then, the reciprocal "knowing" between God and Abraham had a missional purpose: God's commitment to blessing humanity. Spoken against the backdrop of the actual reason for God's presence in this narrative—namely to act in judgment on the degraded wicked-

---

[2]This is the major theme of my book *The Mission of God* (Downers Grove, Ill.: InterVarsity Press, 2006).

ness of Sodom and Gomorrah, these words are a gospel life preserver in a sea of human sin. But they are also so typical of God. God on his way to judgment stops en route with Abraham. Not because he needed a meal, or because Sarah was a better baker than believer, but because it is God's way, in wrath to remember mercy. So God reminds himself of that wider, longer, and ultimately redemptive mission for all nations even at the point of proximate judgment in history. And because Abraham is key to that, God takes Abraham into his confidence. For Abraham, being known by God and knowing God in intimate collegiality, is inseparable from the mission of blessing that motivates the heart and plans of God.

If there is a lesson here for us, as there doubtless is in the narrator's mind in telling the story, it must be that knowing God is never an end in itself but must be pursued within the context of serving the mission of God in bringing blessing to the nations. Knowing God is missional, not merely devotional. Knowing God serves God's purpose of blessing others, not merely our personal enjoyment of being blessed.

2. *Teaching.* Coming to the central phrase in Genesis 18:19, and the nearer of God's expressed purposes in "knowing" (choosing) Abraham, we find a strongly ethical core to balance the missional thrust of the closing phrase. To be the means of blessing to the nations, as God had promised, Abraham must become a great nation. But what kind of nation, what kind of community must it then be?

The narrator is about to show us the kind of society it must *not* be—namely like Sodom and Gomorrah. The contrast at this point is very stark. Having spoken about his purpose in choosing Abraham, God immediately continues, presumably now speaking directly to Abraham,

The outcry against Sodom and Gomorrah is so great and their

sin so grievous that I will go down and see if what they have done is as bad as the outcry that has reached me. If not, I will know. (Gen 18:20-21)

The sin of Sodom is crying out to heaven. *Outcry* is the word that speaks of people crying out for help in the midst of cruelty, oppression and violence. It is the word repeatedly used of the Israelites crying out in Egypt. The rest of what we know about Sodom, from Genesis 19, Isaiah 1 and Ezekiel 16:49, tells us that it was a sink of the most appalling human wickedness, including violence, sexual perversion, inhospitality, bloodshed, injustice, arrogance, affluence and callous neglect of the poor (a rather modern-sounding list, when you compare it with the societies many of us live in).

In contrast to *that,* says God, I have chosen Abraham so that he will initiate and shape a community that will be utterly different: one that will walk in the way of the LORD, not in the way of Sodom; one that will be committed to righteousness and justice, not to perversion and oppression. Already in this text God anticipates the role that Moses will actually later play in giving commands to the people of Israel that would enable them to walk in the ways of the LORD and do righteousness and justice (cf. Deut 4:5-8, 10:12-19). But it all begins in the loins of Abraham (who, we recall with wry surprise, has not even had a son by Sarah yet, let alone a whole "household after him" to instruct).

So a second major purpose of knowing, and being known by, God is the task of passing on the ethical requirements of God, so that his people can fulfill their missional function in the world. The remarkable logic of verse 19 contains three main elements: God's election of Abraham; God's ethical expectation from Abraham and his community; God's mission of bringing blessing to the world through Abraham. Election—Ethics—Mission. And each of the last two are expressed as the purpose of the first. "I have chosen him so that . . . so that . . ." There is no biblical mission without biblical ethics. And there is no biblical election without the matching divine intention— a transformed and transforming community, and a blessed world of nations. And that, says God, is why I know Abraham and he knows me. As Calvin comments:

> Certainly God does not make his will known to us so that knowledge of him should die with us. He requires us to be his witnesses to the next generation, so that they in turn may hand on what they have received from us to their descendants. Therefore, it is a father's duty to teach his children what he himself has learned from God. In this way we must propagate God's truth. It was not given to us for our private enjoyment; we must mutually strengthen one another according to our calling and our faith.[3]

Challenging questions. The more intimate any friendship, the more liberty the friends feel to challenge one another within the bonds of understanding, affection and trust. We see something of this at two points in this rich narrative. Each side throws out a question to the other, which, by its rhetorical nature, presents a challenge and calls for a response. In this way also we see the profound confidence with which God knew Abraham and Abraham knew God.

1. Challenge to faith. The first challenging question in the narrative is addressed to Abraham, but it is about Sarah, so it necessarily involved them both. The subtle narrative begins to disclose the identity of the feasting visitors.

---

[3]John Calvin, *Genesis* (Wheaton, Ill. and Nottingham, U.K.: Crossway Books, 2001), p. 177.

"Where is your wife Sarah?" they asked him.

"There, in the tent," he said.

Then the LORD said, "I will surely return to you about this time next year, and Sarah your wife will have a son."

Now Sarah was listening at the entrance to the tent, which was behind him. Abraham and Sarah were already old and well advanced in years, and Sarah was past the age of childbearing. So Sarah laughed to herself as she thought, "After I am worn out and my master is old, will I now have this pleasure?"

Then the LORD said to Abraham, "Why did Sarah laugh and say, 'Will I really have a child, now that I am old?' Is anything too hard for the LORD? I will return to you at the appointed time next year and Sarah will have a son."

Sarah was afraid, so she lied and said, "I did not laugh."

But he said, "Yes, you did laugh." (Gen 18:9-15)

It was at this point, if it had not happened already, that Abraham and Sarah become aware of who it is they are entertaining. In asking after Abraham's wife, they not only use her name (how did they know it?), but use the new form of the name that God himself had only recently given to her (Sarah, instead of Sarai, see Gen 17:15-16). Then, one of the three speaks words that recall what God had said to Abraham on that same occasion and in almost the same words, about the coming birth of a son.

Sarah's response, as she overhears the news (and she may be hearing it for the first time, since we are not told if Abraham had ever told her what God had told him in Genesis 17), is exactly the same as her husband's when he first heard it. She laughs (cf. Gen 17:17). In both cases it was the laughter of disbelief (not unbelief, but incredulity—the idea seemed impossible). Abraham laughed into the ground, to which he had fallen facedown. Sarah laughed "inside herself" (literally), and ridiculed in her thoughts the idea that a one-hundred-year-old man and a long post-menopausal woman could enjoy sex let alone conceive a baby. Then came the next surprise that clinched the identity of the anonymous speaker. We read that Sarah was inside the tent door which was behind the "man." So she was behind his back. He could not see her, and he had not heard her, for she had laughed and spoken "inside herself." But he had heard the soundless laughter and read the unspoken thoughts and he asks two questions: "Why did Sarah laugh?" and "Is anything too hard for the LORD?"

Sarah was afraid—as well she might be—and her denial was partially true, she had not laughed out loud at least. Her consternation was not just because her inner thoughts had been (somewhat more delicately) repeated aloud—but because it really is a lot to ask of any woman to be confronted with two of the greatest attributes of God in quick succession, his omniscience and his omnipotence, when all she wanted was her siesta. So the episode ends with (I think) almost pantomime comedy over Sarah's laughing; perhaps it even ended with laughter all round. "I didn't laugh." "Yes you did laugh." "No I didn't!" "Yes you did!" And the narrator must be laughing as he tells the story for each occurrence of the word is a reminder that the son who is to be born will actually bear the name *Laughter:* Isaac—in Hebrew, *Yitzhaq,* "He laughs"—(which the narrator exploits to the fullest when he reaches that point in the story, see Gen 21:1-7).

But the question that God addresses to both Abraham and Sarah is the challenge to faith. "*Is anything too hard for the LORD?*" It is a very pointed question, for surely even God doesn't give babies to childless hundred-year-olds. Well, does he? Can he? One can imagine attempting to answer God's question with an oscillating conflict between head and heart. "Well, no, of course. . . . But yes, actually in this case . . .

though not really, I suppose." We recall the honesty of the man who said to Jesus, "I believe; help my unbelief" (Mk 9:24 NRSV). Abraham and Sarah were obedient believers in God already, or else they wouldn't even be where they were, in the land of Canaan. But a son next spring? At this point their laughter shows that "the powerful promise of God outdistances their ability to receive it."[4] What we have here, then, is an encounter in which Abraham and Sarah's knowledge of God, which was considerable already, is stretched beyond the point of apparent possibility by the challenging question of the God of impossibilities. Brueggemann's reflection is worth quoting.

> Once again, this story shows what a scandal and difficulty faith is. Faith is not a reasonable act which fits into the normal scheme of life and perception. The promise of the gospel is not a conventional piece of wisdom that is easily accommodated to everything else. Embrace of this radical gospel requires shattering and discontinuity. Abraham and Sarah have by this time become accustomed to their barrenness. They are resigned to their closed future. They have accepted that hopelessness as "normal." The gospel promise does not meet them in receptive hopefulness but in resistant hopelessness. . . . "Is anything impossible for the LORD?" This question means to refute and dismiss the protests of the hopeless couple. The refutation is not stated as a proposition, assertion, or proclamation but as a question. It comes as a question because the gospel requires a decision. And that decision cannot be given from above. It must come from Abraham and Sarah.[5]

Jesus posed the same challenge to the faith of his disciples, and called

---

[4]Walter Brueggemann, *Genesis* (Atlanta: John Knox Press, 1982), p. 158.
[5]Ibid.

them to live in the light of the right answer (Mt 17:20; Mk 10:27). To know God is to know there are possibilities that lie beyond the bounds of the possible.

2. *Challenge to intercession.* The first challenging question in this encounter, then, is addressed by God to Abraham and Sarah as a challenge to faith. The second challenging question comes from Abraham and is addressed to God as an act of intercession. Actually, of course, it is a series of questions, but they all revolve around the key one in Genesis 18:25: *"Will not the Judge of all the earth do right?"*

> Then the LORD said, "The outcry against Sodom and Gomorrah is so great and their sin so grievous that I will go down and see if what they have done is as bad as the outcry that has reached me. If not, I will know."
>
> The men turned away and went toward Sodom, but Abraham remained standing before the LORD. Then Abraham approached him and said: "Will you sweep away the righteous with the wicked? What if there are fifty righteous people in the city? Will you really sweep it away and not spare the place for the sake of the fifty righteous people in it? Far be it from you to do such a thing—to kill the righteous with the wicked, treating the righteous and the wicked alike. Far be it from you! Will not the Judge of all the earth do right?"
>
> The LORD said, "If I find fifty righteous people in the city of Sodom, I will spare the whole place for their sake."
>
> Then Abraham spoke up again: "Now that I have been so bold as to speak to the Lord, though I am nothing but dust and ashes, what if the number of the righteous is five less than fifty? Will you destroy the whole city because of five people?"

"If I find forty-five there," he said, "I will not destroy it."

Once again he spoke to him, "What if only forty are found there?"

He said, "For the sake of forty, I will not do it."

Then he said, "May the Lord not be angry, but let me speak. What if only thirty can be found there?"

He answered, "I will not do it if I find thirty there."

Abraham said, "Now that I have been so bold as to speak to the Lord, what if only twenty can be found there?"

He said, "For the sake of twenty, I will not destroy it."

Then he said, "May the Lord not be angry, but let me speak just once more. What if only ten can be found there?"

He answered, "For the sake of ten, I will not destroy it."

When the LORD had finished speaking with Abraham, he left, and Abraham returned home. (Gen 18:20-33)

God has honored the intimacy that exists between himself and Abraham by sharing his plans—to go down and see if the wickedness of Sodom is as bad as the outcry against it. This knowledge leads Abraham to initiate a remarkable dialogue with God, as they stand together overlooking the very cities they are talking about. As Gordon Wenham points out, the directness and intimacy of this conversation is all the more highlighted by the fact that this is the very first time in the Bible that any human being *initiates* a conversation with God—previously all divine-human encounters have started with a question or statement by God.[6] And Abraham himself, in his deferential forms of speech, shows that he is aware of the boldness of what he is doing—a fact which in itself also points to the depth of his confidence in his friendship with God.

[6]Gordon J. Wenham, *Genesis 16—50* (Dallas: Word Books, 1994), p. 52.

Nevertheless, though Abraham is the first to break the silence of Genesis 18:22, God himself has created the chink of opportunity which Abraham seizes. "If not, I will know," God had said at the end of his speech about Sodom and Gomorrah. There was just a possibility that things were not quite as bad as they sounded. Perhaps not all the people were as wicked as the rumor that had reached heaven. In allowing for that possibility, God waits to see what Abraham will do with it. And, as God probably wanted and hoped for, Abraham steps into the minimal hope that God has merely hinted at, with bold intercession around the hypothetical possibility that it might be true.

Abraham's problem was focused on the character of God. If God were to destroy the wicked cities totally, would he not then also destroy any righteous that might be there? And would that be consistent with his character? If Yahweh is the universal God who defines what justice means, then surely he must act according to his own justice. It is unthinkable that God should do otherwise, is it not? The rhetorical question makes a categorical declaration: Whatever Yahweh does, will be done, and must necessarily be done, in justice— his own divine, definitive justice. This is not (as sometimes claimed), suggesting that God is himself subject to some higher power or "principle" of justice (which would mean God is less than fully sovereign). Rather it accepts that God defines whatever is just and right, and so God will always act in consistency with his own character.

If that is granted, then what Abraham asks for, and the answers he receives each time from God, are both alike quite remarkable.

3. *A surprising kind of merciful justice.* Take first of all the precise content of Abraham's request. His *premise* was that a just God would not kill the righteous *with* the wicked, as if making no distinction. But his *request* was not, as we might have expected, that

God should therefore distinguish between the two in such a way as to spare or rescue the righteous and destroy the wicked. Rather, he asks that God should spare the whole city *including the wicked,* for the sake of any righteous who were there. In other words, Abraham's questioning seems to subvert the usual human calculus in these things. We tend to think that a few wicked people are all it takes for God to come slamming in with judgment, no matter how many relatively righteous folk are around. Abraham assumes the contrary, that a few righteous people would be all it takes for God to act mercifully toward a whole city full of the wicked. There is something here about Abraham's understanding of God's merciful character that transcends a more abstract calculus of "blind justice" that "gives each his due."

It is hard to dig much deeper into the theological understanding of Abraham at this point, but I cannot help feeling this too has something to do with his knowing God. He has discerned in God a quality of righteousness that goes beyond numbers, scales and mechanical calculation of deserts. He has discerned that there is a *saving* and "protective" power in righteousness that moves the heart and hand of God. God's willingness to spare the wicked for the sake of the righteous is a remarkably different kind of "justice" for the judge of all the earth to be exercising. But there is a trajectory that leads from this insight into the saving potential of righteousness to the cross itself and the way Paul meditates on the perfect righteousness of the one man, Jesus (Rom 5:12-19). On a much later occasion, Ezekiel had to counterbalance this insight against those who wanted to presume upon it and protect themselves from the consequences of their own wickedness by pointing to a few righteous neighbors or family members. That's not the way it works, Ezekiel had to say. God *will* act to punish the wicked, even if the punishment is deferred, and do not try to imagine that you can claim vicarious credit out of somebody else's account (Ezek 14:12-23) and then go on being wicked.[7]

4. A surprising kind of bargaining. But secondly, God's answers to each of Abraham's six queries demonstrate even more clearly something surprising about God's idea of righteousness—consistent with what has just been said.

It is often alleged that this exchange between Abraham and God is a typical piece of oriental bargaining. The context, it is said, is the bazaar, in which buyer and seller will haggle over the price of some object. The buyer offers the lowest price he can think of, to which the seller counters with something much higher. The buyer then makes slightly higher bids, and the seller makes slightly lower offers, until they eventually agree on a price somewhere in between, and shake hands on a satisfactory deal. But if this is the metaphorical background to this exchange between Abraham and God, then it is completely subverted and turned upside down.

Let us imagine that "sparing Sodom" is the "object" that Abraham is trying to "buy." He needs to discover what is the minimum "price" in terms of righteous residents that God will be prepared to accept in exchange for the goods Abraham wants (which, we must remember, is that the whole of Sodom and Gomorrah be spared, not just that Abraham's relatives be rescued). So Abraham starts the bidding: "Would you spare the whole city for the sake of fifty righteous people?" Now if this were a normal bargaining situation, then God would retort with something like, "Oh no, I couldn't do it for only fifty; there would have to be at least a hundred." After which Abraham might have haggled a bit more until some figure in between, such as

---

[7]Cf. Christopher J. H. Wright, *The Message of Ezekiel*, The Bible Speaks Today (Downers Grove, Ill.: InterVarsity Press, 2001), pp. 172-81.

seventy-five, would have been accepted. But on the contrary, and perhaps to Abraham's own surprise, his first offer is immediately and emphatically accepted with a very clear promise—Genesis 18:26. Encouraged by this good news, Abraham proceeds to see if he can get the "price" dropped still further—and every lower figure is equally quickly accepted by God. What is going on here? It is certainly not remotely like typical haggling. It is as if a would-be buyer says, "Let me offer you fifty dollars for that piece of jewelry." And the stall-holder unexpectedly says with a smile, "Sure, you can have it for fifty dollars." So the surprised buyer says, "Would you part with it for forty-five dollars, then?" And the seller says again, "Sure, why not?" And so the buyer goes on offering a *lower and lower* price, gets the same accommodating answer each time, and eventually walks away with the thing for ten dollars. Not, it will be agreed, what normally happens in the marketplace.

But that's the point. This is not the marketplace. This is God, the judge of all the earth, and the impression we get is that, while he must act in punitive justice against the egregious wickedness of So-dom and Gomorrah, nothing would please him more than to be able spare them if even a mere handful of righteous people were there—just as the impression one would get from the reverse haggling de-scribed above is that the seller was really just as keen to give the goods away as the buyer was in asking for them.

In other words, Abraham is learning more about God. Knowing God is taking on new and surprising depths, for he discovers in this intercessory encounter that God is far more compassionate than he ever thought possible. God will go a very long way to spare the wicked. It is almost as if he needs hardly any persuading at all to do so, if only he could. Abraham is already learning what Ezekiel would later put into words on behalf of God:

> For I take no pleasure in the death of anyone, declares the Sovereign LORD. Repent and live! (Ezek 18:32)

> Say to them, "As surely as I live, declares the Sovereign LORD, I take no pleasure in the death of the wicked, but rather that they turn from their ways and live. Turn! Turn from your evil ways! Why will you die, O house of Israel?" (Ezek 33:11)

And in his intercession, Abraham is already mirroring back to God something of God's own compassion and generosity. Certainly he is "reminding" God of the saving power of righteousness. To know God is to reflect God—even to reflect God back to God in intercession. If God grieved over Sodom, even as its wickedness angered him, because of the "cry for help" that was coming up from the city (cf. Job 24:12), then God's emotions found a human heart to lodge in. For even Sodom had Abraham, a man who knew God, as its intercessor.

Remembering a friend. Things did not turn out quite as Abraham prayed for or expected. On the one hand, that is because even the rock-bottom "price" that God accepted at the close of the intercession was not met. Not only were there not *ten* righteous people in Sodom, the narrative of Genesis 19 insists that there was not even *one*. The attack upon the house of Lot after the angelic guests had arrived there included all the men of the city, which is emphasized by the narrator:

> But before they lay down, the men of the city, the men of Sodom, both young and old, all the people to the last man, surrounded the house. (Gen 19:4 NRSV)

Even Lot, who we are told elsewhere had a righteous soul that was disturbed by his surroundings (though not enough to get out earlier; 2 Pet 2:7-8), was not actually a citizen of Sodom, and was explicitly disowned by the rest of the inhabitants (Gen 19:9). So in the end,

God fulfills his threat. The "If not" clause on the clipboard of his angelic fact-finders remained inactivated. It really was as bad as the outcry. There were no righteous inhabitants to stay the execution, or at least postpone it. The judgment must fall.

So we cannot say that Abraham's intercession had been unsuccessful. The simple fact was that not even the minimum condition on which God and Abraham had finally agreed had been met.

However, although Abraham had not asked for it, God did act in merciful deliverance for the relatives of Abraham within the city—the family of Lot. The story need not detain us here, except for the way it concludes.

> So when God destroyed the cities of the plain, *he remembered Abraham,* and he brought Lot out of the catastrophe that overthrew the cities where Lot had lived. (Gen 19:29, italics added)

So the narrator makes a clear connection between the intercession of Genesis 18 and the rescue of Genesis 19. God acted. But as he acted, he "remembered Abraham"—as you do with your friends. Only this was not merely a casual memory. It implies that the *way* God acted and *the result* of God's action were both materially affected by Abraham's engagement in prayer with the God he knew so intimately. We may never plumb the depths of mystery that surrounds how God's sovereign action in history is connected to the prayers of God's people, but the Bible simply affirms that the link is there. "God destroyed . . . God remembered . . . God brought out."

Abraham knew his God, and God remembered his friend.

Moses—God's Servant

Abraham, as we saw, is called "God's friend." He is also once described as "God's servant" (Gen 26:24). That is a term which is not nearly so common in the Old Testament as we have made it in popular Christian circles to describe almost any faithful Christian in any form of Christian ministry (and why not, of course?). It was, rather, a term of high honor reserved for a very select few of the great figures of the Old Testament story. It is most often used of David (e.g., 2 Sam 7:5; 1 Kings 11:13; Ezek 34:23), but also of Caleb (Num 14:24), Job (Job 1:8), Isaiah (Is 20:3), and Zerubbabel (Hag 2:23)—and of course the mysterious Servant of the Lord in Isaiah 40—55. The most outstanding, however, is undoubtedly Moses. Moses is called the servant of the LORD at the moment of his greatest triumph, the crossing of the Reed Sea (Ex 14:31), and at the moment of his mountain death and burial (Deut 34:5).

Moses' intimacy with God. It is not only from the sparing use of the term by the narrator, however, that we learn about Moses, the LORD's servant. God himself uses the term in a most illuminating divine testimony to the intimate relationship between God and Moses. Moses' sister and brother, Miriam and Aaron, had spoken against him, claiming equality with him in prophetic gifting and challenging the exclusiveness of Moses' right to be the sole spokesperson for God. God summoned the three siblings to his presence and then defended Moses (who had refused to defend himself) with these words:

> When a prophet of the LORD is among you,
>> I reveal myself to him in visions,
>> I speak to him in dreams.
> But this is not true of my servant Moses;
>> he is faithful in all my house.
> With him I speak face to face,
>> clearly and not in riddles;
>> he sees the form of the LORD.

Why then were you not afraid
to speak against my servant Moses? (Num 12:6-8)

God acknowledges that there was an "ordinary" level of genuine prophetic revelation that he mediated through dreams and visions to others. But with Moses there was a direct revelatory encounter that took place "mouth to mouth" (literally), in which Moses saw "the form" of God (a term which suggests, not that Moses saw God directly—something denied elsewhere—but that he certainly had some kind of visual experience of the presence of God). Other texts describe how this direct intimacy between Moses and God was "as a man speaks with his friend" (Ex 33:11), and even had physiological effects on Moses, noticeable to the people—his face shone with the reflected glory of God (Ex 34:29-35).

From Moses' side, it is made clear that this was something he sought and longed for. Indeed, though it's hard to believe—even after his encounter at the burning bush, his prolonged embodiment of the mighty power of God in the plagues and at the crossing of the sea, his forty days alone with God at the top of Mount Sinai, and his breathtakingly successful engagement with God on behalf of the people immediately afterwards—Moses still feels he does not know God well enough and wants more! In some ways, this is starting at the wrong end of our story, but it is a key point for our purpose of exploring what it means to know God.

Listen to Moses wrestling with God and asking to know him more. Some people are just never satisfied.

> Moses said to the LORD, "You have been telling me, 'Lead these people,' but you have not let me know whom you will send with me. You have said, 'I know you by name and you have found favor with me.' If you are pleased with me, teach me your

ways *so I may know you* and continue to find favor with you. Remember that this nation is your people."

The LORD replied, "My Presence will go with you, and I will give you rest."

Then Moses said to him, "If your Presence does not go with us, do not send us up from here. How will anyone know that you are pleased with me and with your people unless you go with us? What else will distinguish me and your people from all the other people on the face of the earth?"

And the LORD said to Moses, "I will do the very thing you have asked, because I am pleased with you and I know you by name."

Then Moses said, "Now show me your glory." (Ex 33:12-18, italics added)

The elements of Moses' desire are clear. He picks up God's affirmation that God is pleased with him and knows him by name, and says, in effect, "Well if that is so, teach me your ways. I want to know who you really are and how you operate" (as if he didn't know?). And when God promises to send his Presence (literally, his Face) to accompany the people, Moses retorts, in effect, "You'd better; how else will the world know that we are any different from other nations if you are not among us?" And when God says, "Fine, I'll do what you ask, because I am pleased with you and know you by name," Moses fires his climactic request, "Show me your glory, then!"

It is an amazing short interchange, displaying a great depth of familiarity and boldness, and yet still longing for more. Knowing God, for Moses, was not some static daze of mystical bliss. It was an ongoing, ever-deepening journey into the heart of God, with "negotiations and love songs" along the way.

But we need to return to the start of the story to savor the encounter that has just preceded this intimate exchange.

Space for grace. As in Genesis 18—19, the context is one of gross sin and threatened judgment. The Israelites had rebelled against God immediately after the making of the covenant, while Moses was on Mount Sinai receiving the law from God. With Aaron's collusion they had made a golden image of a calf-bull, and then compounded their idolatry with immorality and revelry (Ex 32:1-6).

As Moses and Joshua come down the mountain, God speaks these terrifying words, threatening to destroy this whole people and start again with Moses.

> "I have seen these people," the LORD said to Moses, "and they are a stiff-necked people. Now leave me alone so that my anger may burn against them and that I may destroy them. Then I will make you into a great nation." (Ex 32:9-10)

In the encounter between God and Abraham in Genesis 18, we pondered the way God left a chink of opportunity, with the words, "but if not, then I will know," about the evil report on Sodom. And that hint of an invitation was enough to set Abraham interceding. In a very similar way here, there is a mysterious quality about God's words to Moses, "Now leave me alone . . ." Had Moses already started to interject to calm God's anger? Did God hope that he would? In any case, why did God need to say anything at all to Moses in this way, and declare his intention? Why did need to stop off for a meal with Abraham on his way to Sodom and chat about his intentions? The fact is, of course, that God had no need whatsoever to pause in this way on either occasion. God could have poured out his anger from above on Sodom or on the Israelites with no warning given to anybody. But on both occasions, God pauses to share his intention, and on both occasions God inserts a phrase that hints at an invitation for

his human conversation partner to object or suggest other considerations. God leaves space for grace, scope for hope. Both Abraham and
Moses know God well enough to pick up the hints and clues. Both
jump to intercession. That's what people do, who know God.

More challenging questions. The primary account of Moses' intercession is Exodus 32:11-14 (it is recalled again in Deut 9).

> But Moses sought the favor of the LORD his God. "O LORD," he
> said, "why should your anger burn against your people, whom
> you brought out of Egypt with great power and a mighty hand?
> Why should the Egyptians say, 'It was with evil intent that he
> brought them out, to kill them in the mountains and to wipe
> them off the face of the earth?' Turn from your fierce anger; re-
> lent and do not bring disaster on your people. Remember your
> servants Abraham, Isaac and Israel, to whom you swore by your
> own self: 'I will make your descendants as numerous as the stars
> in the sky and I will give your descendants all this land I prom-
> ised them, and it will be their inheritance forever.' " Then the
> LORD relented and did not bring on his people the disaster he
> had threatened. (Ex 32:11-14)

There are three questions expressed or implied in Moses' prayer
here. All of them are addressed to the heart of God, and what most
matters to him.

1. What about your covenant? "Your people, whom you brought out
of Egypt," says Moses. This is the language of God's covenant commitment to Israel. In Deuteronomy the sharpness of this point is
brought out more clearly, in Moses' reminiscence of this terrible moment. Listen to God virtually disowning the people, as if to say—
"this is your lot, Moses, not mine."

Then the LORD told me, "Go down from here at once, because *your* people whom *you* brought out of Egypt have become corrupt. (Deut 9:12, italics added)

And then listen to Moses' riposte, as if to say, "Sorry, God, but they are your people and it was you, not me, who brought them out of Egypt; I wasn't even very keen on the idea, as you may recall."

I prayed to the LORD and said, "O Sovereign LORD, do not destroy *your* people, *your own* inheritance that *you* redeemed by *your* great power and brought out of Egypt with a mighty hand. (Deut 9:26, italics added)

All through the preceding months, God had been reaffirming his covenant commitment to Israel, and had just ratified it with a prolonged ceremony and celebration meal in Exodus 24. Moses was not about to let God back away from that commitment now. So he boldly reminds God of it.

2. *What about your reputation?* We saw in chapters two and three that the exodus had been a massive demonstration, to Israel and Egypt alike, of the identity and power of Yahweh. They, and other nations, knew something about this incomparable God from what he had done in that great act of liberation of his people from slavery.

What would these other nations now think and say if Yahweh wiped the Israelites out in the wilderness? They would treat such news with utter mockery. Either Yahweh is malicious, they would scoff, (he only got them out of slavery in order to kill them anyway!), or he is incompetent and can't complete the job (cf. Num 14:16, where Moses deploys the same argument on another occasion of threatened destruction). Malicious and/or incompetent—is that the kind of reputation Yahweh wanted to be circulating around the Middle East? Moses knew what we know from the rest of the Old Testament, that God is passionately concerned for the honor of his own name. So here, he urges God to think twice before he acts precipitately and ruins his own reputation. Strong stuff, but powerfully effective. So effective, in fact, that Ezekiel later tells us that God thought a lot more than twice in restraining the full extent of his anger with Israel, precisely for the sake of his name (Ezek 20). And when he did finally pour it out in the exile, the result was such a massive degradation of his name among the nations, that he acted to restore them back to their land, for the same reason (Ezek 36:16-23).

3. What about Abraham? Moses saves the most powerful argument to the end. God's promise to Abraham occurs many times in Genesis, but Moses picks out, through his choice of words in Exodus 32:13, the particular occasion that is recorded in Genesis 15. It was then that God had promised descendants as numerous as the stars in the sky. And more importantly, it was then that God had gone on oath, by a kind of "self-curse" ritual of severed animals. This oath was confirmed explicitly as God swearing "by myself" in Genesis 22:16. So God had, in effect, put his own life and existence "on the line" in his promise to Abraham. His oath means, "As surely as I am God, and will continue to be God, I will keep this promise; if I fail, I cease to be God."

Now God had made an amazing alternative proposal to Moses: "I will destroy *these* people, but I will not abandon the plan for which I brought them into existence—that is, to bring blessing to all nations, as I promised Abraham. So I will do it through *you and your descendants*. Abraham will be history. It will be the Children of Moses now. Turn the clock back to Genesis 11. We'll start all over again" (see Ex 32:10; cf. Num 14:12).

Far from being tempted by such a proposal, Moses shrinks in

shock at the thought, and virtually rebukes God for even suggesting it. *"What about Abraham, and your promise to him?* You can't go back on that without breaking your own oath, sworn on your own life. God, this isn't even an option."

This is an astounding piece of intercession. The paradox of it is that, in appealing to God to change the plan he has just announced, Moses is appealing to God to be consistent with the plan he had declared long ago. Intercession is not so much trying to change the mind of God as to engage with the deepest purpose of God and seek to align events and outcomes in the present to the known will of God. Above all, it shows how profoundly Moses knew God. He wasted no time trying to elicit divine sympathy for *Israel* ("they didn't really mean it;" "I have been away a long time, it's not surprising"). Rather he went straight to the heart of the things that really matter *to God*— his covenant, his name, his mission to the nations. All these would be gravely endangered if God were to destroy the people completely in his anger.

Moses knew his God.

And God knew his Moses.

Perhaps he'd better think it through again.

Grace abundant. So we return to Moses, after the worst is over, virtually pestering God for a deeper knowledge and clearer vision of the very glory of God. What would God do in response for his doughty and persistent servant? We return to where we left off above, with Moses asking to see God's glory. Instead, God offers to show him his goodness, to proclaim his name, and to let Moses see "his back." All very mysterious, but a defining moment in Old Testament history and theology, when we hear God's self-identification.

And the LORD said, "I will cause all my goodness to pass in front

of you, and I will proclaim my name, the LORD, in your presence. I will have mercy on whom I will have mercy, and I will
have compassion on whom I will have compassion. But," he
said, "you cannot see my face, for no one may see me and live."

Then the LORD said, "There is a place near me where you may
stand on a rock. When my glory passes by, I will put you in a
cleft in the rock and cover you with my hand until I have passed
by. Then I will remove my hand and you will see my back; but
my face must not be seen." (Ex 33:19-23)

Then the LORD came down in the cloud and stood there with
him and proclaimed his name, the LORD. And he passed in front
of Moses, proclaiming, "Yahweh, Yahweh, the compassionate
and gracious God, slow to anger, abounding in steadfast love
and faithfulness, maintaining steadfast love to thousands, and
bearing wickedness, rebellion and sin. But he will not neglect
due punishment, visiting the wickedness of fathers on children
and children's children to the third and fourth generation."

Moses bowed to the ground at once and worshiped. (Ex
34:5-8, author's translation)

- Moses asked to know God, and God responds. When giving the
  Ten Commandments, he had sanctioned the second command-
  ment (against idolatry) with the threat that God visits the sin of fathers on children to the third and fourth generation (which effectively confines the effect of sin and punishment within the living
  family of the perpetrator in a multigenerational family culture[8]),

---

[8]That is to say most Israelite households included three or four living generations from grandfather to youngest sons. If the head of the household committed idolatry, the whole family
would be sucked into it, and so the whole family "'to the third or fourth generation'" would
suffer the effects of it.

but followed by the promise of God's steadfast love to *thousands* [of generations] of those who love him (Ex 20:5). Now, in the wake of the great apostasy at Mount Sinai, God reverses the order of that combination. His limitless love (there have scarcely yet been a thousand generations in all human history) is put first, and the unavoidable realities of temporal punishments and their effect on connected generations within families is included as sad necessity. God cannot simply overlook sin indefinitely. But his choice is to "bear" it—that is to "carry" it in forgiving grace. And that in turn depends on what God puts at the very top of his identity card—words that entered into the definition of the character of Yahweh throughout the rest of the Old Testament.[9]

Yahweh, Yahweh, the compassionate and gracious God, slow to anger, abounding in steadfast love and faithfulness. (Ex 34:6, author's translation)

Moses asked God to show him his *glory*. God said he would show him his *goodness*. Here is the definition of both. To know God is to know *this* God, the God of compassion, grace, love and faithfulness.

CONCLUSION

What, then, have we learned about knowing God from these two great Old Testament saints, Abraham and Moses?

In both cases, it is said that God knew them—that was the basis of whatever dimensions of knowing God they then enjoyed. To paraphrase John, in a way he would probably approve, we know God because he first knew us.

---

[9]The echoes, or direct quotations, of this verse can be seen all over the Old Testament, e.g., Num 14:18; Deut 5:9-10; 1 Kings 3:6; Neh 9:17; Ps 86:15; 103:8, 17; 145:8; Jer 32:18-19; Lam 3:32; Dan 9:4; Jon 4:2; Nahum 1:3.

In both cases, there was an intimacy with God that enabled an astonishing degree of forthright conversation, and meaningful dialogue. These were intensely personal relationships in which strong things could be said in the context of total trust.

In both cases, it is clear that God takes very seriously what his friend and his servant say to him. There is no sense that either conversation was all pre-scripted, or a big bluff. Knowing God means engaging in a relationship that has integrity and respect on both sides.

In both cases, knowing God involved being taken into God's confidence as regards God's plans and purposes. There is a privilege and a responsibility in seeking to interpret the times in the light of the known word and will of God and with the mind of Christ, through his Spirit.

In both cases, the knowledge that God was about to act in judgment on the wicked brought not a flicker of gloating or anticipation of something long overdue. Rather it led to urgent intercession on behalf of those who stood, deservedly, in the blast-path of God's wrath. For those who know God, the knowledge of God's wrath is as distressing as the Scriptures say it is to God himself.

For Abraham, knowing God meant challenging him in relation to his justice, and learning that God was surprisingly willing to spare the wicked, while relentlessly powerful in his judgment on rampant, unrepentant and incorrigible evildoers.

For Moses, knowing God meant challenging him in relation to his covenant, his name and his promises, and finding that the way to stay God's hand was through God's heart, where those realities were eternally enthroned.

For us, the lesson most probably is that, in the adventure of knowing God, there are depths of prayer that we have scarcely begun to paddle in.

6

Knowing God Through Reflecting His Justice

Jeremiah's prophecy of the new covenant is familiar—perhaps mainly because it is quoted twice in the letter to the Hebrews.

> "This is the covenant I will make with the house of Israel
>   after that time," declares the LORD.
> "I will put my law in their minds
>   and write it on their hearts.
> I will be their God,
>   and they will be my people.
> No longer will a man teach his neighbor,
>   or a man his brother, saying, 'Know the LORD,'
> because they will all know me,
>   from the least of them to the greatest,"
>   declares the LORD.
> "For I will forgive their wickedness
>   and will remember their sins no more." (Jer 31:33-34)

"They will all know me, from the least of them to the greatest" (Jer 31:34). What does this mean? Most explanations and most sermons (including some of my own in the past) say that this promises a close personal relationship of every individual believer with the Lord, as part of the spiritual reality of the new covenant. In contrast to the alleged distance of the individual from God in the Old Testament, we are enabled in the New Testament, through the indwelling Holy Spirit, to know God personally and intimately, and without the mediating teaching of priests or leaders.

Now I will not for a moment deny that a close personal relationship with God is a very precious truth of Christian experience made possible for us through Christ's blood of the new covenant. But is this what Jeremiah was talking about when he spoke about knowing God? Supposing we could ask Jeremiah what he meant by this phrase "then they will know me," I think the long-suffering prophet (or perhaps his faithful scribe Baruch) would have answered, "Have you not been listening? I have explained *twice already* in my book what it means to know God. Try paying attention to my words."

For indeed, in Jeremiah 9:23-24 and 22:13-17, we have passages in which "knowing God" is not only referred to in a pivotal way, but virtually defined for us as well. In 9:23-24, knowing God is compared with the best gifts that God offers people and is found to surpass them. In 22:13-17, knowing God is contrasted with the worst wickedness that a recent king in Israel had embodied. And in both passages, we shall find, the flavor is distinctly practical and ethical, and scarcely "spiritual" or devotional at all. So apart from any other considerations, the following study is a small exercise in the importance of reading Bible texts in the light of their own immediate context, and not importing assumptions that are really from other parts of the Bible, or (more often) other vague and general aspects of Christian faith.

KNOWING GOD IN COMPARISON WITH THE BEST GIFTS OF GOD

> "Let not the wise man boast of his wisdom
>   or the strong man boast of his strength
>   or the rich man boast of his riches,
> but let him who boasts boast about this:
>   that he understands and knows me,
> that I am the LORD, who exercises kindness,
>   justice and righteousness on the earth,
>   for in these I delight,"
>   declares the LORD. (Jer 9:23-24)

Jeremiah 9:23-24 is a beautifully crafted and balanced little poem. It is rather like a see-saw, or a pair of scales, with a central pivot and things balanced on either side. The central pivot, according to God who is speaking, is "knowing me."

Then on one side of that central pivot the prophet places three things that human beings value:

- wisdom
- strength
- riches

While on the other side, he places three things that God values:

- kindness
- justice
- righteousness

God's good gifts and their perversion. Jeremiah 9:23 is rather surprising—as much to us as doubtless to Jeremiah's hearers. All three things listed are highly valued good gifts of God. Elsewhere in the Old

Testament these things are praised, commended, given thanks for. So Jeremiah is not talking here about some swaggering tycoon boasting of ill-gotten gains and throwing his muscle around. Wisdom, strength and wealth are all presented in the Old Testament as good gifts of God. They are not evil things in themselves, but can be signs of blessing.

1. *Wisdom.* The word means applied knowledge; the discernment that comes from experience of life; the combination of sharp insight and well-honed skills; the ability to understand deeply and to act accordingly. It is repeatedly commended in the book of Proverbs as the most valuable thing you can and should set your heart on. It is the fruit of a life lived in the fear of the LORD—that is by taking God seriously and living according to his ways and standards. So biblical wisdom is not just intellectual, but also profoundly spiritual (it comes from relationship with God), and ethical (it is exercised in moral obedience to God). The young and newly appointed king Solomon, when he was given a chance to ask God for anything, asked for wisdom to do justice in his government, and was highly congratulated by God for doing so (even though the tragic irony of his reign shows that he squandered the gift and turned it into a nice little earner for his personal wealth and glory).

2. *Strength.* This normally means simple physical vigor—whether the normal strength of able-bodied men (and it usually is men), or sometimes abnormal strength given by God. The remarkable vigor of Moses, which enabled him to climb mountains at 80 and again at 120, and scan the horizon with undimmed eyesight, is noted with clear narrative pleasure. Samson of course is more ambiguous, but his great strength is certainly attributed to the Spirit of Yahweh. And in the Psalms, even if there is a bit of a moan that it all wears out for most of us around 70 or 80, physical vigor is a thing to be prayed for and celebrated.

3. *Riches.* Wealth can, of course, be the fruit of wickedness, oppression, theft and injustice. But it need not be. And there are clear cases of those we could call the righteous rich in the Old Testament, people like Abraham, Boaz and Job—as well as the anonymous figures whose righteous and generous use of wealth is commended in texts like Psalm 112, or Proverbs 31. God's will for his people was not perennial poverty, but abundance enjoyed with justice, compassion and generosity.[1]

So here is a little list of things that most Old Testament Israelites would have placed in a basket of positive goods. These were some of the ingredients of a life lived under the covenant blessing of God. Those who could be called wise, or strong, or rich, had nothing to be ashamed of—provided these qualities were acquired and exercised within the framework of covenant obedience.

But Jeremiah says—*Do not boast of these things.* For what happens when we do? Boasting means that we take credit for ourselves what are in reality gifts of God, and then turn them into matters of pride and self-glory. That in turn quickly perverts the good gifts themselves into cruel vices that usually issue in moral evils of all kinds. This is a temptation that Deuteronomy recognized very early on and warned Israel about even before they entered the land. The rich fertility of the land would give Israelites every opportunity to increase their wealth in crops, oil, wine, herds and flocks, etc. Then, says Moses,

You may say to yourself, "My power and the strength of my hands have produced this wealth for me." (Deut 8:17)

And that indeed is the self-made man's boast—claiming all he has accumulated as his own exclusive achievement and for his own ex-

---

[1]Jonathan J. Bonk, "Righteous Rich," in *Missions and Money: Affluence as a Missionary Problem—Revisited* (Maryknoll, N.Y.: Orbis, 2006).

clusive benefit. There is no dispute that he has put in effort and strength. The question is where did *they* come from? Where did you get your strength, your abilities, your intelligence, your energy, the very breath you breathe?

> But remember the LORD your God, for it is he who gives you the ability to produce wealth. (Deut 8:18)

But when people ignore this warning, then all three of the good gifts are corrupted into horrible parodies of what God intended them to be as blessings.

- Wisdom, as a matter of boasting, becomes intellectual arrogance, which is often characterized as "folly" in the Wisdom literature.

- Strength, as a matter of pride, ends up as violence, aggression, grasping from others by the use of oppressive and unjust power. Bullying can be an individual or a national trait, and both are ugly abuses of strength.

- Riches, when accumulated out of covetous greed, turn to excess, extravagance and "conspicuous consumption," and generate the horrendous injustice of exploitative wealth existing side by side with degrading poverty.

So then, these are good but dangerous gifts. And the main danger lies in the temptation to boast of them and thereby pervert them into terrible evils. And, says the prophet, a very powerful counterweight to that temptation is to understand that there is something far better than any or all of them by comparison. It is a good thing to enjoy the gifts of God. It is a far better thing to know the Giver himself. And so "knowing God" becomes the pivot of the whole poem. If you are going to exult and glory in something—don't do it in relation to the lesser things that God gives. Do it on account of your relationship with God himself. But that will lead to a very different kind of "boast-ing."

For, to know God means to share in his concerns, understand his scale of values and priorities, and to take delight in what pleases him—as is true of any genuine human relationship as well.

God's delights and their practice.

> I am the LORD who exercises kindness,
>   justice and righteousness on earth
>   for in these I delight. (Jer 9:24)

Here is the second group of three, this time not blessings of God that humans value, but actions of God that he values, and delights in when he sees them imitated.

1. Kindness. The Hebrew word is *hesed,* and kindness is a slightly weak translation for it. It is a very strong word, speaking of commit-ted faithfulness within a relationship, a commitment which is willing to take on costs or burdens for the sake of the other party, and to do so for the long haul. So it certainly includes the element of kindness, but exercised as an act of unselfish love, out of a strong sense of bonding. It is characteristic of God's faithfulness to his covenant promises—and therefore saturates the Psalms, where it is celebrated repeatedly. It is translated, "unfailing love," "lovingkindness," "faith-fulness," etc. As a human characteristic, it is modeled in the book of Ruth. Ruth is commended for her remarkable *hesed* to the family of her widowed mother-in-law Naomi, and her own deceased husband. Similarly Boaz is commended for his *hesed* to Naomi's family by ful-filling the duties of a kinsman-redeemer, at cost to himself.

2. Justice. The Hebrew word is *mishpat.* It is the act of putting things right for those who are wronged, whether (normally) through legal action on their behalf, or even through military action at times (as in the case of the "judges"). It is an active word—not just a concept or ideal. It means taking up the case, or the cause, of those who are weak or vulnerable and acting to rectify their suffering.

3. *Righteousness.* The Hebrew word is *tsedaqah.* It has at heart that which is straight and true, that which is truly what it ought to be. When used of human relationships it means when people behave to each other in the way that God wants—in fairness and compassion, in making sure that the weak are upheld and the strong restrained. Our translation "righteousness" is somewhat too abstract and conceptual, and a bit moralistic. *Tsedaqah* in Hebrew is not a concept. It is what you do, or what governs what you do.[2]

These, then, are the things that God "delights in" when they are done "on earth" (not just in heaven), for they reflect his own character. He is the God of all faithfulness (Deut 32:4). Righteousness and justice are the foundations of his throne (Ps 97:2). So these things bring him the same pleasure and joy that parents have when they see something of themselves in their children (at least the better traits).

We should savor that phrase, "in these I *delight.*" This is not just a matter of a list of "divine attributes" or "ethical duties" that we can coolly list and contemplate. This verse uses the language of emotional response. What brings a smile to the face of God? To what circumstances does God respond with the exclamation, "That's utterly delightful!"? What warms his heart? Answer, when he sees acts of committed love among people; when he sees people achieving justice for others; when he can affirm that a situation has been put right in his eyes—"On earth as it is in heaven." Nothing is or remains perfect

---

[2]On these ethical terms in the Old Testament, see Christopher J. H. Wright, *Old Testament Ethics for the People of God* (Downers Grove, Ill.: InterVarsity Press, 2004), esp. chap. 8 on justice and righteousness.

like this in a fallen world, of course. All our efforts are partial. But this verse encourages us to believe that God takes genuine pleasure in even faulty and provisional efforts that are truly characterized by these qualities. This must not be confused of course, with the false idea that we can achieve or deserve our salvation through our own righteousness (which, Isaiah reminds us, is nothing more than filthy rags, if we place such saving expectations on it). Rather this is to say that the God of all justice and righteousness is pleased with the attitude and behavior of those who share his commitment to such qualities and behavior.

How did Israel know this? From where did they get the idea that Yahweh their God was passionately concerned about kindness, justice and righteousness, in doing them and delighting in them? From the very beginning of their own story as a nation. What else is the story of the exodus but a massive demonstration of God's faithfulness to his promise to Abraham, not only in rescuing Israel from Egypt but in persevering with them through their appalling behavior in the wilderness? God's dealings with Pharaoh were an exercise in justice—putting down the oppressor and liberating the exploited. And God's law at Sinai provided Israel with a pattern of social righteousness which, had they observed it, would have made them the object of admiring questions to the surrounding nations (Deut 4:6-8).

But more than these historical demonstrations of God's character, there is the self-identification that God makes to Moses at Sinai. When Moses presses Yahweh to show himself, God does not provide an awesome visual cosmic show that might challenge the computer graphics of a Hollywood spectacular. No, he hides Moses, and allows him only to see "his back" (whatever that mysterious phrase means). But God does speak. And what words he speaks—a proclamation of Yahweh's own name that resonates through the consciousness of Israel through all the generations of Old Testament history and literature.

> Yahweh, Yahweh, the compassionate and gracious God, slow to
> anger, abounding in love and unfailing commitment (*hesed*),
> maintaining love to thousands, and carrying wickedness, rebel-
> lion and sin, yet not failing to visit the guilty. (Ex 34:6-7, my
> translation)[3]

But even before that God had made a similar point to Abraham,
about the kind of community he wanted, in line with his own character. After enjoying a meal with Abraham and Sarah, God (who was
at that moment on his way with two angels to mete out judgment on
Sodom and Gomorrah), reminds himself of the purpose for which he
had called this man:

> Abraham will surely become a great and powerful nation, and
> all nations on earth will be blessed through him. For I have cho-
> sen him, so that he will direct his children and his household
> after him to keep the way of the LORD by doing what is right
> and just (*tsedaqah,* and *mishpat),* so that the LORD will bring
> about for Abraham what he has promised him. (Gen 18:18-19)

The mission of Israel then, as a people taught these things since
Abraham, was to be a community of righteousness and justice, in the
midst of a world like Sodom characterized by cruelty (note the "outcry" of Gen 18:20-21), perversion, arrogant affluence and callous neglect of the poor (Ezek 16:49). Israel was to walk in the way of the
LORD in a world walking in the way of Sodom. To be the people of
this God, Yahweh, was to know what kind of life this God required
and to walk in it. It still is.

---

[3]See chap. 1 n. 1 and chap. 5 n. 9 for a list of references through the Old Testament that quote
these verses.

So for us to claim to "know God," means a lot more than a vague, or even an intense, subjective spiritual experience. It means to know *this* God, the God who calls for, who longs for, who delights in, the exercise of love, justice and righteousness. Are these things our delight also? If they are among his top priorities, are they also among ours? For if they are not, then it is not *this* God we know, but some other god more comfortable and congruous with our own predilections.

What then do we learn from Jeremiah's exquisite mini-poem on knowing God in Jeremiah 9:23-24? First it reminds us of a point that is very familiar, but easily forgotten: that knowing God in personal relationship is more important and precious than enjoying any or all of his blessings in themselves. Wisdom, strength and riches can all be wonderful blessings, and whatever measure of them comes our way should be received with humble thanksgiving as gifts from our heavenly Father's hand.

Second, we are reminded that boasting in them is the fastest exit route from the personal joy of knowing God. Why is that? Mainly, I think, because all three of these things, when we take credit for them ourselves, generate pride, and pride is the number one poison, the impenetrable roadblock to knowing God. We easily puff up with pride in educational achievement and qualifications (and we don't make it easier when we identify and introduce other people with adulation for their stratospheric degrees, as if that was a measure of their spiritual stature as well). Our culture glories in sporting prowess, and the cult of the body-beautiful easily pollutes healthy Christian affirmation of the body into something much more deceptive and destructive. And of course greed, gluttony and avarice are still among the deadly sins, for this very reason—they are deadly to our relationship with God.

Perhaps that is why all three are subtly subverted in the New Testament, even as they are still affirmed as gifts. Not many, said Paul, among the Christians at Corinth, had been "wise" in the world's eyes. Not many were among the powerful and wealthy. It was the weak, the poor and the apparently foolish that God had chosen and called to himself.

But thirdly, we recall that when we obey the word of Jesus, and "seek first the kingdom of God and his righteousness/justice," then these gifts of God can be ours as well—but on God's terms and for God's glory, not ours, and never as a matter of boasting.

You need wisdom?

> If any of you lacks wisdom, he should ask God, who gives generously to all without finding fault, and it will be given to him. (Jas 1:5)

You need strength?

> He said to me, "My grace is sufficient for you, for my power is made perfect in weakness." Therefore I will boast all the more gladly about my weaknesses [was Paul thinking of Jeremiah 9:23 when he wrote this?], so that Christ's power may rest on me. . . . For when I am weak, then I am strong. (2 Cor 12:9-10)

> I can do everything through him who gives me strength. (Phil 4:13)

You need money?

> I have learned to be content whatever the circumstances. I know what it is to be in need, and I know what it is to have plenty. I have learned the secret of being content in any and every situation, whether well fed or hungry, whether living in plenty or in want. . . . And my God will meet all your needs ac-

cording to his glorious riches in Christ Jesus. (Phil 4:11-12, 19)

KNOWING GOD IN CONTRAST TO THE WORST EVIL OF HUMANITY

Jeremiah lived through the reigns of several kings. Two of them stood in stark contrast to each other. Josiah was a godly young king, only a little older than Jeremiah himself. But he died young in battle (that was a mystery of providence in itself, and Jeremiah grieved for him, it seems). Jehoiakim, who followed him, was the exact opposite, and yet had a long reign in which Jeremiah suffered increasing unpopularity and persecution for his critical outspokenness. Jeremiah 22:13-17, in the midst of a chapter that is an edited collection of several of Jeremiah's sayings in relation to the kings of Judah, is a powerful comparison of these two kings. And in it comes a sharp and uncompromising definition of what knowing God means. The words that follow were addressed to Jehoiakim.

> "Woe to him who builds his palace by unrighteousness,
>   his upper rooms by injustice,
> making his countrymen work for nothing,
>   not paying them for their labor.
> He says, 'I will build myself a great palace
>   with spacious upper rooms.'
> So he makes large windows in it,
>   panels it with cedar
>   and decorates it in red.
> "Does it make you a king
>   to have more and more cedar?
> Did not your father have food and drink?
>   He did what was right and just,

so all went well with him.
He defended the cause of the poor and needy,
    and so all went well.
Is that not what it means to know me?"
    declares the LORD.
"But your eyes and your heart
    are set only on dishonest gain,
on shedding innocent blood
    and on oppression and extortion." (Jer 22:13-17)

The contrast. What a catalog of wickedness we read in these verses. Jehoiakim stands accused by the prophet of

- exploitation of workers for low or no wages (something prohibited in the law Deut 24:14-15)

- conspicuous affluence and consumption (second stories and windows were uncommon in normal homes; cedar was the most expensive kind of wood; red dye was the most expensive form of paint; and what was wrong with the palace of Solomon that Jehoiakim needed to build a new one?)

- fraud and greed

- bloodshed, violence and murder

- oppression and extortion

This is a picture of the abuse of governmental power and privilege that is all too familiar in the modern world too. And not just among notoriously corrupt regimes in the majority world. All of the above can be laid on the charge sheet of some western governments and corporations in the way they deal with the poorer world.

By contrast, Jeremiah gives a very short and simple description of the reign of Josiah, in Jeremiah 22:15-16.

- He did righteousness and justice (which God delights in).
- He defended the poor and needy (whom God cares for).

And so, comments Jeremiah, "It was *good* for him." He was good. His reign was good. Things were good, under a king who put God's priorities above his own selfishness.

And then come the startling words at the end of Jeremiah 22:16.

"Is not this to know me?" saying of Yahweh. (Jer 22:16, author's translation)

I find this a remarkable statement, and an infinitely challenging one. For in the midst of all our spiritualizing, pious, devotional, even mystical, verbosity over what "knowing God" is all about, here is a stark four-word question (in Hebrew) that stands like a lighthouse on a rock in the middle of a tossing sea of words. We come wondering how to steer a course toward truly knowing God, and here we find a biblical, prophetic, inspired, luminous, *definition* of what knowing God is. Its simplicity and clarity defies all obfuscation. Doing righteousness and justice; defending the poor and needy—*that* is to know God. Where does this leave our limp evangelical pietism, or our suspicion of all forms of social engagement, or the rationalizations by which we excuse ourselves from the ideological and practical battlefields of economics and politics? We do not all have Josiah's calling into political authority. But if we wish to be among those who know God and are worthy of his verdict—"good," then we had better share Josiah's commitment to social justice and action for the poor and needy.

The source. How did Josiah come to know God in this essentially practical commitment to social justice? From God's law. The most notable event in the reign of Josiah was the rediscovery of the Book of the Law during the restoration of the temple (2 Kings 22). Josiah was already committed to the reformation of the faith of Judah, and this discovery accelerated his commitment and the reforms. Very probably the book that was discovered was, or included, what we now know as the book of Deuteronomy. Imagine listening to such words as these being read in your royal hearing. And notice how they link affirmations about what Yahweh is like and what he typically does, with what he wants his people to do.

> For the LORD your God is God of gods and Lord of lords, the great God, mighty and awesome, who shows no partiality and accepts no bribes. He defends the cause of the fatherless and the widow, and loves the alien, giving him food and clothing. And you are to love those who are aliens, for you yourselves were aliens in Egypt. (Deut 10:17-19)

So this is exactly what Josiah set out to do. He learned about the justice and compassion of Yahweh in the Scriptures, and then determined to imitate them in his own life, and to inculcate them in the social life of the nation. That's how, according to Jeremiah, he *knew* Yahweh—by doing what Yahweh did, and by implementing what Yahweh wanted to be done.

We are told very little about Josiah's inner spiritual life, other than that he had come to seek the God of his father David early in life (2 Chron 34:3)—possibly referring to a kind of personal conversion experience, in the wake of the whole generation of evil led by his grandfather Manasseh and his father Amon. But we *are* told about his intentional obedience to the law with its deep saturation with concern for the poor and needy, the marginalized and vulnerable—the widow, orphan and alien. As a result, Josiah goes down in the record as the only Israelite king in the whole Old Testament who gets an unsullied A+ on his ethical report card. This is the verdict of the historian (who was also imbued with the spirit of Deuteronomy).

> Neither before nor after Josiah was there a king like him who turned to the LORD as he did—with all his heart and with all his soul and with all his strength, in accordance with all the Law of Moses. (2 Kings 23:25)

Josiah, in short, knew the LORD. And the proof was practical and ethical. And the affirmation that he did know the LORD, came not from his own boasting, but posthumously from God himself through his prophet.

CONCLUSION

In the light of both these texts, then, how can we claim to know God?

Not on the basis of boasting of the things that we *have*—however good they may be, and however much they are in themselves the gifts and blessings of God.

Nor, indeed, on the basis of anything we might *say,* boastingly or not. For we recall that Jesus warned us that, "Not everyone who *says* to me, 'Lord, Lord,' will enter the kingdom of heaven" (Mt 7:21).

Nor, either, on the basis of the great things we allege we that we *do* in ministry. For not all such claims are authentic or demonstrate that those who profess them actually know God are owned by Christ. Jesus added the following warning:

> Many will say to me on that day, "Lord, Lord, did we not prophesy in your name, and in your name drive out demons and perform many miracles?" Then I will tell them plainly, "I never knew you. Away from me, you evildoers!" (Mt 7:22-23)

These are sobering words. Who would you think has a better

claim to know God than someone who has a prophetic ministry? Or someone who has a great deliverance ministry in the name of Christ? Or someone who performs miracles of healing (probably) in the name of Christ? Surely these great ministries are proof of knowing God? Not necessarily, says Jesus. There will be *many*, Jesus says, who do these things without knowing God at all. There will be many who appear to have the most spectacular ministries, but at the end of the day, Jesus will not own them, and will have to say: "We don't know each other. I never knew you. So it follows that you never knew me."

No, the only real test, according to Jesus is doing "the will of my Father who is heaven" (Mt 7:21). And what is that? Jesus endorsed, and modeled, all that the Old Testament said about Yahweh's care for the poor, his passion for justice and compassion. And if those things were the will of Yahweh, then they are certainly included among "the will of my Father." And so Jesus includes among the beatitudes a blessing on "those who hunger and thirst for righteousness/justice." The ones who will be owned and welcomed by "The King . . . my Father" will be those who fed the hungry, showed hospitality to the stranger, clothed the naked, cared for the sick and visited the prisoner (Mt 25:34-36).

James, whose letter possibly comes the closest in the New Testament to reflecting directly the ethos of the teaching of Jesus, asserts (and note the explicit relating of his point to God "our Father"):

Religion that God our Father accepts as pure and faultless is this: to look after orphans and widows in their distress and to keep oneself from being polluted by the world. (Jas 1:27)

Sadly, many of us are rather more keen on the latter (keeping ourselves unpolluted by the world) than on the former. Or we are very adamant on preserving the purity of the faith and sound doctrine. But James goes on:

> What good is it, my brothers, if a man claims to have faith but has no deeds? Can such faith save him? Suppose a brother or sister is without clothes and daily food. If one of you says to him, "Go, I wish you well; keep warm and well fed," but does nothing about his physical needs, what good is it? In the same way, faith by itself, if it is not accompanied by action, is dead. (Jas 2:14-17)

John agrees.

> This is how we know what love is: Jesus Christ laid down his life for us. And we ought to lay down our lives for our brothers. If anyone has material possessions and sees his brother in need but has no pity on him, how can the love of God be in him? (1 Jn 3:16-17)

Or how, we might add, can the knowledge of God be in him either.

All these are deeply challenging verses—to me as much as to any reader. And I have included these New Testament passages intentionally to show that the kind of sharp demands of practical social ethics we read in Jeremiah and Deuteronomy are not merely Old Testament obsessions that our more spiritual New Testament faith has left behind. The Bible speaks with one voice on this.

There is no true knowledge of God without the exercise of justice and compassion.

I have to ask myself, then, what is there in my life that shows any love for, and practical commitment to, the poor and the needy? God may not have called me to direct hands-on involvement in a social ministry, but whatever else I do for a living, can I see that God's concern for the weak and the poor is reflected at all in my praying, thinking, giving and doing? For according to the measure of my answer is the measure of my knowing God.

Josiah did righteousness and justice.

He defended the cause of the widow and orphan.

"Is that not what it means to know me?"
   declares the LORD. (Jer 22:16)

7

Knowing God Through
Returning to His Love

I once saw a church poster that said:

"You can never get rid of love.
The more you give it away,
the more it keeps coming back."

Hosea would have agreed. He is sometimes called "the prophet of love," not only because he speaks about love a lot, but also because God demanded of him an amazing act of costly personal love in which the message of his book was fleshed out in his own suffering. And he also discovered something of the returns of love—the love that God commanded him to show by welcoming back an unfaithful but returning wife, and the love that God longed to show to an unfaithful people if only they would return to him.

But it would be equally accurate to describe Hosea as the prophet of the *knowledge of God,* for this is something he talks about even more often than love. In fact the Hebrew verb and noun for "know" and "knowledge" occur about a dozen times in this book of only fourteen chapters (English translations sometimes use different words to render the same Hebrew word, such as "acknowledge," "care for," "realize" or "recognize," but even so, the emphasis is clear). So Hosea certainly deserves his place in any book about knowing God. And more than that, he speaks about how God knew Israel as a son and wanted to relate to them as their Father, so Hosea doubly deserves his place in this book about knowing God the Father through the Old Testament. So we turn to his book, anticipating some rich and challenging teaching about what it means to know God.

If you list all the passages in Hosea that speak about knowing God, or the knowledge of God,[1] they fall roughly into three categories:

• the knowledge of God that Israel enjoyed through their experience of God's redemption (with some additional aspects to what we studied in chapter two above);

• the lack of the knowledge of God that Hosea observes among his contemporaries, manifested in spiritual rebellion and moral collapse throughout society; and

• the restored knowledge of God that Hosea looked forward to, if only the people would return to God in repentance that was genuine and not a superficial mouthing of the old litanies.

These, then, are the three main sections of our study in this chapter.

KNOWLEDGE OF GOD GAINED THROUGH REDEMPTION

Knowing God as Savior.

> Yet I have been the LORD your God
>   ever since the land of Egypt;
>   you know no God but me,
>   and besides me there is no savior. (Hos 13:4 NRSV)

---

[1]If you want to read them all together (which is well worth pausing to do), they include Hos 2:8; 2:20; 4:1; 4:6; 5:4; 6:3, 6; 8:2; 9:7; 11:3; 13:4-5 (and cf. the last verse of the book, Hos 14:9). All the references in this chapter are to the verse numbering in English Bibles. The numeration in the Hebrew text is often somewhat different.

This verse, like Hosea 2:15 and 12:9, take us back to the exodus. That was when God had made himself so clearly known to the Israelites as Yahweh. That was when he had claimed them for his own and entered into exclusive covenant relationship with them. In chapter two we explored this in considerable depth and marveled at the curriculum of knowledge of God that Israel gained through the experience of God's saving grace and power. What we see again here is that, for Hosea too, the knowledge of God is not something mystical or esoteric. It is historical and experiential. Israel knew Yahweh because of his redeeming action, and they also knew that no other god had acted in that way. Accordingly, their unique experience generated unique knowledge of the unique God.

The language of this verse in Hosea has been strongly influenced, obviously, by the opening of the Ten Commandments.

I am the LORD your God, who brought you out of Egypt, out of the land of slavery. You shall have no other gods before me. (Ex 20:2-3)

Israel was to *have* no other gods because they *knew* no other gods. This does not mean, of course, that the Israelites did not know that other nations had other gods—they had just been delivered from Egypt, a land of very powerful deities whose names they knew well. It means that Israel had covenant allegiance to Yahweh alone as their savior and Lord, and must not dissipate that loyalty by going after such other gods. The experience of God's salvation carries with it the immense privilege of knowing who the living God is, and the immense responsibility of living in complete loyalty to him alone. To know God in this sense is to be committed to him.

Hosea goes on in the following verse to make the knowledge between Israel and God a mutual thing:

I *knew you* in the wilderness,
> in the land of burning heat. (Hos 13:5, author's translation
and italics)

Most English translations (but not the KJV) obscure Hosea's balanced phrasing by translating "I knew you," as "I cared for you," or "I fed you"—which redundantly anticipates Hosea 13:6. Hosea's point is that Israel's knowledge of God is related to, and dependent on, God's knowledge of Israel (a point we saw earlier in the personal relationship between God and both Abraham and Moses). Those whom God calls to know him are those whom God himself knows—with all the personal, relational, pastoral and reassuring implications of that truth. Here the point is national; in Psalm 139 it is profoundly personal.

Israel, then, knew God as a privilege that resulted from the way God had rescued them from slavery and cared for them in the wilderness. Through these primary events and experiences Israel knew their God and God knew his people. This is the essence of the covenant relationship—a relationship which, as we shall soon see, was being severely threatened by Israel's behavior.

Hosea goes on to portray the redemptive covenant relationship between Israel and Yahweh by means of two powerful human metaphors: husband-wife, and father-son. Israel knew God (or should have done), as a wife knows her husband and as a son knows his father.

Knowing God as husband. We need to go right back to the beginning of the book of Hosea, and back to the personal experience out of which his whole message was shaped. Prophets in Israel were not unfamiliar with some very bizarre instructions from God in relation to the way they were to illustrate or act out their message, but this book opens with one of the most shocking things any prophet ever heard God tell him to do.

When the LORD first spoke through Hosea, the LORD said to Hosea, "Go, take for yourself a wife of whoredom and have children of whoredom, for the land commits great whoredom by forsaking the LORD." So he went and took Gomer daughter of Diblaim, and she conceived and bore him a son. (Hos 1:2-3 NRSV)

The NRSV here preserves the shock of the triple repetition of the Hebrew word for the behavior of a prostitute, which the NIV somewhat dissipates by its variation of "adultery" and "unfaithfulness."

God's words here have caused commentators (and devout readers of all ages) considerable problems. Did God tell Hosea to do something that was, strictly speaking, contrary to the law of Moses? Prostitutes were not supposed to be tolerated in the land at all, let alone taken in marriage. If so, it must have been a terribly difficult and shaming thing for Hosea to be obedient to such a command.

Some people soften the matter by reading the verses "proleptically." That is to say, the editorial record of God's command to marry Gomer anticipates what actually happened later (that she was unfaithful to him and turned to prostitution) *as if* it had been part of the original instructions. Hosea didn't know at the time that this is how it would turn out—even if God did. Well, that is possible (we know that Hebrew sometimes expressed as a purpose something that we would more normally express as a result). But it seems better to me to take the words at face value. God told Hosea to go and take an unlawfully practicing prostitute as his lawfully wedded wife. It may be shocking and hard to believe, but so was the behavior of Israel that Hosea was called to address.

Now, in the rest of Hosea 2—3, it is clear that Gomer represents Israel and Hosea represents Yahweh, so that the human story of marriage, unfaithfulness and restoration becomes a living parable of the fraught but redeemable relationship between God and Israel. If Israel, then, were meant to know Yahweh because of what he had done for them, what should Gomer have known about Hosea from his action in taking her as his wife? That is an element in the analogy being presented to us in this prophetic combination of actions and words. Once again it is important to remind ourselves that whatever Gomer came to know about Hosea resulted from what Hosea actually *did*. Hosea did not join a society to debate the social evils of prostitution. Nor did he theorize about possible strategies for the uplift of fallen women. Nor did he simply complain about prostitutes, or even merely take pity on them.

He went and married one.

The same is true in any account of how we can come to know God. It is not through a process of speculation about what God may or may not be like. Nor is it a matter of merely checking off doctrinal checkboxes about God's attributes. God the Son was not content either merely to discuss with his Father possible strategies for amelioration of the human condition, or to send a cosmic sympathy card telling us "I share your pain."

He came and died to save us.

Knowing God means knowing what *God* has done, knowing it was done *for me,* and knowing the *response* I should make.

Gomer would have known, from Hosea's action toward her, that he loved her (this is mentioned as something that he was told to do "again" in Hosea 3:1, implying that it had been part of the original marriage); that he was willing to forgive her past life, or at least not let it stand in the way of their marriage; that he wished to rescue her from that past life; that he had chosen her in particular to marry in this way (since there were doubtless many others in similar circumstances); that he knew her by name (it is significant that she is named in the narrative); that he was prepared to trust her and provide for her (cf. Hos 2:8), up until her repeated unfaithfulness (evidenced in children that Hosea knew were not his own) led to a separation filled with grief and anger.

All of these mirrored the way Israel should have known Yahweh, in reflecting on what he had done for them in taking them to himself in covenant relationship. And indeed Hosea hints at the initial joy and delight of the relationship

> When I found Israel,
>   it was like finding grapes in the desert;
> when I saw your fathers,
>   it was like seeing the early fruit on the fig tree. (Hos 9:10)

Jeremiah picked up this thought as he pictures Yahweh nostalgically thinking back to the wilderness period as a kind of honeymoon period:

> Go and proclaim in the hearing of Jerusalem:
>
> "I remember the devotion of your youth,
>   how as a bride you loved me
> and followed me through the desert,
>   through a land not sown." (Jer 2:2)

When you recall the actual stories of Israel's behavior in the wilderness in the books of Exodus and Numbers, it is clearly a shocking comparison. Both these prophets are saying that the abysmal depravity of the nation in their own day made the wilderness era seem like a honeymoon by comparison!

Knowing God as Father. Hosea 11:1-4 is a sustained metaphor,

comparing Israel's relationship to God with a son to his father. Since
Hosea's prophecy is dominated by the initial marriage metaphor, this
section is all the more interesting.

> When Israel was a child, I loved him,
>   and out of Egypt I called my son.
> The more I called them,
>   the more they went from me;
> they kept sacrificing to the Baals,
>   and offering incense to idols.
> Yet it was I who taught Ephraim to walk,
>   I took them up in my arms;
>   but they did not know that I healed them.
> I led them with cords of human kindness,
>   with bands of love.
> I was to them like those
>   who lift infants to their cheeks.
>   I bent down to them and fed them.[2] (Hos 11:1-4 NRSV)

The theme of knowing God in this way is implied, even though
only negatively, in Hosea 11:3. Sadly, Israel did not know what they

---

[2]Hosea 11:4 is translated in different ways. I have chosen the NRSV here because it assumes that
the metaphor of a father's relationship with a child continues through this verse, which I think
is probably Hosea's intention. Some scholars (and cf. the NET) think that the metaphor has
changed in this verse to Israel as an ox, being led gently by its owner with a leather rope, who
lifts the yoke from its neck and bends down to feed it. The NIV mixes this metaphor into Hos
11:4b. It is possible to translate "cords of human kindness" and "bands of love" as "ropes of
leather" (the Hebrew word *ahabah*, normally translated "love" can mean "leather" in a very few
contexts; it is a homonym—i.e., a word that is spelled the same but can have completely different meanings, such as "party" or "match" in English). Hosea does compare Israel to a young
ox elsewhere (Hos 4:16; 10:11). So the ox metaphor is possible here. However, in my view it
seems more likely that the son-father metaphor is being continued.

   I remember my Hebrew professor in Cambridge, commenting on the possibility that *ahabah*
in Hos 11:4 might mean leather rather than love and saying wryly that perhaps we should then
translate Hos 11:1 as "When Israel was a child, I leathered him."

should have known—namely that it was Yahweh who was caring for their interests as their fatherly God.

The themes we find built into Hosea's picture here are similar to the fatherly portraits of God we enjoyed in chapter one. The historical reality that is being referred to yet again, of course, is the exodus and wilderness experience and all the events that fill that narrative. And these events are being here portrayed as the action of a father for a child in need. The strength of the father is made available in gentleness and love toward the child. As we also saw in chapter five, the affirmation that Israel was Yahweh's firstborn son was made even before the exodus (Ex 4:22), as a reason for God's demand that Pharaoh should release him. But here the picture is not so much the issue of the rights of a firstborn and the claims of the divine Father over against the oppressor who is depriving the firstborn of his legitimate inheritance. Rather it is simply the picture of a loving and caring father that is to the fore.

What, then, were the fatherly actions of God that Israel should have known, as listed in this short parable of their history? Some very human and familiar parental actions are listed to illustrate God's relationship to his people:

- He loved them and called them to himself, as a father calls a child to his side. The tragedy was that his fatherly calling was met with incorrigible refusal and increasing distance.

- He taught them to walk. That is a patient parental process that involves a lot of falling down too, and Israel's multiple fallings tested the patience of God again and again.

- He took them up in his arms—the action of a father when a child is tired, or stumbling, or in some danger. The early history of Israel is replete with such actions by God on Israel's behalf.

- He healed them (cf. Ex 15:22-26)—even if they refused to acknowledge that it was Yahweh who did it. On occasion, by contrast, they hankered after the more healthy diet, as they thought, that they had enjoyed in Egypt (Num 11:4-6).

- He led them, as a father leads a child to safety, out of the murderous regime of Egypt.

- He lifted the yoke from their necks (if the NIV is to be preferred to the NRSV in Hos 11:4)—another clear allusion to the exodus; or (if NRSV is preferred), he lifted them into close intimacy with himself.

- He stooped down to feed them—literally at ground level in the case of the manna and quails.

These things are celebrated also in Deuteronomy 8, which is echoed by Hosea in several ways, and with the same perception of the fatherly nature of all that God did for Israel at that time of their history (Deut 8:5).

Here, then, as savior, husband and father, is the God whom Israel knew, and these are the ways in which God had acted precisely so that they could know him. They were to know God through faithfulness as of a wife to a husband, and through obedience as of a son to a father. But the tragedy that Hosea observed was a people who should have known God in all these ways rejecting and suppressing that knowledge, and doing so to such an extent that Hosea could make the astonishingly absolute diagnosis, "there is no . . . knowledge of God in the land" (Hos 4:1 NRSV).

KNOWLEDGE OF GOD LOST THROUGH REBELLION

Hosea gives us a number of clues as to how it was that a people who were unique among all the nations in being entrusted with the knowledge of God (cf. Deut 4:32-39) came to be a people lacking not only the true knowledge of God but even any true insight into their own desperate plight (Hos 5:4; 7:9). The primary cause was the idolatrous seduction of the Canaanite fertility cults, likened to marital unfaithfulness, in which they refused to acknowledge the gifts they had received from Yahweh and even attributed them to other gods (Hos 2:5-8). A second cause was their refusal to live by the moral standards that God had established for their society in the Ten Commandments, and the infection of every area of social life with rampant evil (Hos 4:1-3). And a third cause was a total failure of moral leadership on the part of those who were supposed to be the teachers of the nation (Hos 4:4-6).

In other words, the knowledge of God was lost because the people persistently failed to acknowledge God's gifts, to walk in God's ways, and to teach God's laws. As we turn to consider each of these, we will find that there are sharp lessons here for the people of God in any era.

Failure to acknowledge God's gifts. As far as we can tell, Hosea was the first to use the metaphor of marriage to portray the relationship between Yahweh and Israel. It was a remarkably bold step to take in the context of the strongly sexual nature of the cult of Baal that he was opposing. It really is a case of stealing your enemy's guns. In the Canaanite fertility cult, the male god Baal had his female consort Asherah. Their sexual prowess mirrored and guaranteed the fertility of nature—of the soil, of your animals, and of your women. So the worship of these deities included the visible representations of standing stone pillars (the phallic symbol) and wooden poles or trees (as the female symbol). Israel had been told to destroy these things completely and have nothing to do with the religious practices that went along with them (Deut 7:5; 12:30-31). Those practices included sacralized sexual acts with religious prostitutes that were believed to foster fertility in the natural realm (described in Hos 4:10-14).

So Hosea was confronted with the Israelites falling into the Canaanite myth of the sacred marriage of the gods, in order to sustain their need for agricultural abundance and other natural blessings. They went after these other gods, thinking that it was the gods of the land and its Canaanite inhabitants who obviously were the custodians of material prosperity and family fortunes. These were the gods who needed a bit of persuasion and collaborative sexual prodding to get them to unload the good things of life. Not only was this a denial of the fact that it was actually *Yahweh*, the Creator and controller of every natural process, who had always given them all good things richly to enjoy, it was also a terrible act of disloyalty to their covenant Lord. Hosea's boldness lies in the way he chose to counter this perversion—namely by taking over the sexual imagery of Canaanite fertility cults and transforming it into a vehicle to expose the horror of what Israel's sin was doing to them to and God.

Baal, the god of Canaan had his wife—Asherah. Yahweh too has a wife, announces Hosea. But the wife of Yahweh is not some goddess in the mythical world. No, Yahweh's wife is *his own people Israel,* in the real world of human history. Yahweh and Israel are bound together in a covenant relationship that was intended to be as lovingly exclusive as the human marriage bond. For that reason, Israel's behavior in going after other gods (and also, as we read in the rest of the book, in going after political alliances with other nations, which involved religious deals with their gods also), was as grievous, hurtful and disloyal to Yahweh as was Gomer's behavior in reverting to prostitution and bearing illegitimate children after accepting the status and benefits of being Hosea's wife. In both cases it was a shattering breach of trust that justified the baffled grief and anger of the offended partner.

In the transition from the narrative of Hosea 1 to the poetic form of God's address to Israel in Hosea 2, we move from the betrayed marriage of Hosea and Gomer to the broken covenant of God and Israel. The language sustains the metaphor, however, as Israel is addressed as a wife whose unfaithfulness has been exposed and denounced.

> Their mother has been unfaithful
>   and has conceived them in disgrace.
> She said, "I will go after my lovers,
>   who give me my food and my water,
>   my wool and my linen, my oil and my drink."
>
> She has not acknowledged that I was the one
>   who gave her the grain, the new wine and oil,
> who lavished on her the silver and gold—
>   which they used for Baal.
> Therefore I will take away my grain when it ripens,
>   and my new wine when it is ready.
> I will take back my wool and my linen,
>   intended to cover her nakedness. (Hos 2:5, 8-9)

The accusation is clear. Israel went after her "lovers." This is a *double entendre,* since it refers of course to the gods of the Canaanites, but included the actual sexual rituals involved in their fertility cults. The sexual language is both metaphorical and literal. They did this in order to ensure agricultural fertility and sufficiency. Then, when they got those good things, they attributed them to the Canaanite gods, refusing to acknowledge the hand of Yahweh from whom in fact they received them. "She has not *acknowledged*" is literally "she did not *know.*" Again, we remember that this did not mean Israel no longer even knew the name of Yahweh. It means that they refused to acknowledge him in one of his most basic activities—the regularity and fruitfulness of the created order and the fertility of the land that he himself had given to them.

Ingratitude to God for all his good gifts leads to losing the knowledge of God. When we are tempted to attribute to other causes whatever measure of blessing comes our way in life, or even to claim credit for it ourselves, then we are on the dangerous road of forgetting the Lord.

> You may say to yourself, "My power and the strength of my hands have produced this wealth for me." But remember the LORD your God, for it is he who gives you the ability to produce wealth. (Deut 8:17-18)

Failure to walk in God's ways.

> Hear the word of the LORD, O people of Israel;
> > for the LORD has an indictment against the inhabitants
> > > of the land.
> There is no faithfulness or loyalty,
> > and no knowledge of God in the land.
> Swearing, lying, and murder,
> > and stealing and adultery break out;
> > bloodshed follows bloodshed.
> Therefore the land mourns,
> > and all who live in it languish;
> > together with the wild animals
> > > and the birds of the air,
> > > even the fish of the sea are perishing. (Hos 4:1-3 NRSV)

What happens when a whole people refuses to know the God who is their savior, husband and father? What Hosea observes is a complete moral collapse of society and accompanying detrimental ecological effects. He brings this as "an indictment." The language is deliberately legal. The prophets often used the imagery of the law-court as a way of challenging Israel to face up to the serious consequences of their behavior. And it is particularly appropriate here because the accusation includes the breaking of several of the central commandments of Israel's covenant law.

The phrase "no knowledge of God" stands like a pivot between, on the one hand, two other things that were absent from the land, and six things that the land was filled with instead. Yahweh is the God of all truth, trustworthiness and faithfulness, and the God of unfailing covenant love. These things are summed up in two words by Hosea—*emeth* and *hesed*. But since the people had lost all effective knowledge of Yahweh, there was a corresponding loss of these essential characteristics in society as well. No knowledge of Yahweh leads to breakdown of all trust and commitment.

Modern echoes abound. It is not necessary for everybody in a society to be a Christian for there to be some level of truth and loyalty. But there does need to be some collective agreement on transcendent values that demand such qualities of behavior between citizens and neighbors. In the case of the west, that transcendent role was filled for centuries with something akin to the biblical God, even if grossly distorted in the popular mind. Once even the caricature of deity loses any imperative grip on the social conscience, then the bonds of social truthfulness, trust, love, mutual commitment and kindness, all begin to dissolve under the acids of egocentric skepticism.

Instead of such godly characteristics, observes Hosea, the land is filled with the dismal fruit of moral disorder, the breaking of almost all the commandments in the second table of the Decalogue: abusive and violent language; public and private untruthfulness; crimes against life and property; a culture of rampant violence. No knowledge of God leads to no restraints on evil. Paul's searing commentary on this in Romans 1 and 2 expands Hosea's diagnosis of eighth-century Israel into a penetrating analysis of the human condition, once the suppression of the knowledge of God has worked like poison through human society.

Failure to teach God's laws. But who was really to blame? Well, of course, all the Israelites bore their share of blame for the social malaise to whatever extent they participated in it. But Hosea refuses to tolerate a frenzy of mutual accusation. He knows exactly where the primary responsibility lay and pointed his prophetic finger at the group within society to whom God had entrusted the task of teaching the people—the priests.

> Yet let no one contend,
> > and let none accuse,
> > for with you is my contention, O priest.
> You shall stumble by day;
> > the prophet also shall stumble with you by night,
> > and I will destroy your mother.
> My people are destroyed for lack of knowledge;
> > because you have rejected knowledge,
> > I reject you from being a priest to me.
> And since you have forgotten the law of your God,
> > I also will forget your children. (Hos 4:4-6 NRSV)

We are familiar with the sacrificial work of the priests of Israel. They received the sacrifices of the people, performed appropriate rituals with the blood, and declared atonement. Not so well known, however, is the fact the priests were ordained to be teachers of God's law to the rest of the people. This was a vital part of the two way direction of their ministry as mediators—middlemen who acted on behalf of the people before God, and on behalf of God before the people.

Through the priest's handling of the sacrifices, people could come into the presence of God.

Through the priests teaching of the law, the knowledge of God would come to the people.

The commission to teach God's law was part of the ordination mandate given to Aaron and his sons in Leviticus. God said to them:

> You must distinguish between the holy and the common, between the unclean and the clean, *and you must teach* the Israelites all the decrees the LORD has given them through Moses. (Lev 10:10-11, italics added)

This role is also seen as belonging to the whole tribe of Levi in the blessing that Moses spoke in relation to it.

> He teaches your precepts to Jacob
>   and your law to Israel.
> He offers incense before you
>   and whole burnt offerings on your altar. (Deut 33:10)

The fact that the Levites were commissioned and (in better times) trained to do this explains why they feature in programs of scriptural re-education at times of great reformation and renewal in the history of Israel. Jehoshaphat employed them, for example, in an overhaul of Israel's judicial system (2 Chron 19:8-10). Ezra used them to translate and explain the law to the ordinary people (Neh 8:7-8). Sadly, however, they seemed to have abdicated this responsibility more often than they fulfilled it. Hosea is not the only prophet who complains that the priests were not teaching the people. Centuries later Malachi makes the same accusation. Speaking of Levi, and thus of the priests as a class, Malachi says:

> "True instruction was in his mouth and nothing false was found on his lips. He walked with me in peace and uprightness, and turned many from sin. For the lips of a priest ought to preserve knowledge, and from his mouth men should seek instruction— because he is the messenger of the LORD Almighty. But you have turned from the way and by your teaching have caused many to stumble; you have violated the covenant with Levi," says the LORD Almighty. "So I have caused you to be despised and humiliated before all the people, because you have not followed my ways but have shown partiality in matters of the law." (Mal 2:6-9; see the whole section 2:1-9)

The clear implication of these texts is that, although nothing excuses people from their own responsibility in doing wickedness, there is an even higher level of responsibility and blame for those who are supposed to teach the Word of God to the people of God, but who fail to do so. And both Hosea and Malachi address devastatingly serious words from God to such failed teachers of the knowledge of God. Not surprisingly, James warned Christians not to be over-keen to take on the role of a teacher among God's people. It is an enormous calling, but it carries corresponding exposure to the potential judgment of God if our teaching leads people astray or fails to lead them in the ways of God (Jas 3:1).

The absence of good teaching and the danger of false teaching have been twin problems throughout the history of God's people, of course—not only in Old Testament Israel but all down the centuries of the church. In our day the failure of those who claim to be, or are commissioned to be, teachers of God's people seems to have reached epidemic proportions. In the west there are those who teach, practice and bless sexual lifestyles and relationships that are explicitly declared in the Bible to be displeasing to God. While all over the world, but especially in the majority world, the so-called "prosperity gospel" with all its "sanctified" selfishness and covetousness, along with the arrogant affluence of those who presume to teach it from the Bible as "what God wants," deceives millions and grieves the one who called us to self-denying humility and service.

Sex and money. Baal reloaded. The temptations of the Canaanite religion are alive and well today and just as infectious among God's people as in the Israel of Hosea's day. And Hosea's message is still as devastatingly relevant. Those whose false teaching or failure to teach the truth encourages Christians to indulge in ways of life that are ethically disobedient and displeasing to God must bear the greater guilt before God for the absence of the knowledge of God and the corresponding presence of so many moral and spiritual evils.

KNOWLEDGE OF GOD RESTORED THROUGH REPENTANCE

The root of Israel's problem, then, was that they had lost the knowledge of God, as savior, as husband, as father—for all the reasons and in all the ways outlined above. Their only hope lay in recovering that knowledge, in coming back to the God they should have known, in being restored to the relationship they had so grievously betrayed. As God called on Hosea to rebuild the relationship with Gomer, so God intended to rebuild his relationship with his people, as a bridegroom wooing his bride once more. But before that happy restoration could be consummated, Israel had hard lessons to learn about what true repentance really meant. What was involved in returning to God and his love? Once again we need to look at some passages in the body of Hosea's prophecy before returning to the great message based on his marriage in Hosea 2.

The repentance that God wants. At first sight Hosea 6:1-3 sounds very promising—exactly what we longed to hear. Hosea is quoting what the people are saying, and it sounds like they want to come back to knowing God, in just the way Hosea has been saying they have failed.

> Come, let us return to the LORD.
>> for it is he who has torn, and he will heal us;
>> he has struck down, and he will bind us up.
> After two days he will revive us;
>> on the third day he will raise us up,
>> that we may live before him.
> Let us know, let us press on to know the LORD;
>> his appearing is as sure as the dawn
> he will come to us like the showers,
>> like the spring rains that water the earth. (Hos 6:1-3 NRSV)

What the people say here clearly follows on from the concluding verses of chapter 5. There God had accused both the northern and southern kingdoms, Ephraim (meaning the northern kingdom of Israel) and Judah, of turning to Assyria for help. They had become aware of their social, moral and spiritual sickness, but they were turning to the wrong doctor. So God threatens to tear them to pieces until they return to him, admit their guilt, and seek his face. The language of 6:1-3 echoes this—mostly. Surely now at last they are singing the right tune?

Not yet, says God. To our surprise, God seems to dismiss these words of apparent repentance as shallow and fickle.[3]

> What shall I do with you, O Ephraim?
> 　What shall I do with you, O Judah?
> Your love is like a morning cloud,
> 　like the dew that goes away early. (Hos 6:4 NRSV)

The Israelites thought God would come back like refreshing rain. God ironically says that Israel's words of repentance are like mist and dew in the morning—very nice while they last but gone as soon as the day warms up. What is missing? Two things: specific confession of guilt and awareness of the need for forgiveness, on the one hand; and radical ethical change, on the other.

1. Confession of guilt. The one thing that is lacking from the fine words in Hosea 6:1-3 is what God required in Hosea 5:15—"until they admit their guilt." There is no admission of guilt, no acknowledgement of specific wrongdoing in Hosea 6:1-3. Rather, it is simply assumed that God will restore the people and they will know him again—without dealing with the causes of the alienation.

Yet none of this (Hosea 6:1-3) is enough. The crucial requirement of "admitting their guilt" (Hos 5:15) has been omitted. They have faced their woundedness (Hos 6:2; cf. Hos 5:12-13) but not their waywardness. Healing is sought, even resurrection, but no specific sin is mentioned. This absence of repentance and failure to confess

---

[3]The view of the majority of commentators is that Hos 6:1-3 must be read, in the light of the immediately following verses, as an inadequate litany of repentance. Francis I. Andersen and David Noel Freedman, however, accept it at face value as a sincere expression of repentance. But this necessitates removing it from its present context between Hos 5:15 and Hos 6:4, and seeing it as a later response of the people: "5:12-15 and 6:4-6 together come before 6:1-3 logically, and in time" (Francis I. Andersen and David Noel Freedman, *Hosea: A New Translation with Introduction and Commentary,* Anchor Bible [New York: Doubleday, 1980], p. 426). But if one retains the present order of the text it is hard to avoid the impression that Hos 6:4 is an implied rejection of the sincerity and efficacy of Hos 6:1-3.

sins by name contrast sharply with Hosea's closing song of penitence (Hos 14:1-3).[4]

There, in Hosea 14:1-3, Hosea frames words of repentance that explicitly acknowledge the guilt and sin of idolatry. And furthermore, he asks the people not only to repent of it, but to renounce it altogether; to stop idolizing military muscle (a very modern idolatry still) by recognizing that such "gods" can never be stronger than the human hands that made them.

> Return, O Israel, to the LORD your God.
>> Your sins have been your downfall!
> Take words with you
>> and return to the LORD.
> Say to him:
>> "Forgive all our sins
> and receive us graciously,
>> that we may offer the fruit of our lips.
> Assyria cannot save us;
>> we will not mount war-horses.
> We will never again say 'Our gods'
>> to what our own hands have made,
>> for in you the fatherless find compassion." (Hos 14:1-3)

The repentance that God seeks, then, is one which clearly recognizes sin and renounces it, and on that basis asks for forgiveness. Anything else fails to grapple with the roots of our predicament. But when repentance meets God's criteria, then his response is immediate:

---

[4]David Allan Hubbard, *Hosea,* Tyndale Old Testament Commentaries (Downers Grove, Ill.: InterVarsity Press, 1989), p. 125.

> I will heal their waywardness
> > and love them freely,
> > for my anger has turned away from them. (Hos 14:4)

2. Radical ethical change. Ironically, the Israelites rejected Hosea's accusation that they no longer knew God. On the contrary, they protested, they were the people who *did* know God! Wasn't that what distinguished Israel from the surrounding nations? It should have been, but what Israel had forgotten was that to know God meant to walk in his ways. It meant reflecting his character. It meant an ethical commitment to do good. So Hosea starkly contrasts their claim and their practice—and depicts the inevitable judgment that such discrepancy would bring upon them.

> Israel cries to me,
> > "My God, *we—Israel—know you!*"
> Israel has spurned the good;
> > the enemy shall pursue him. (Hos 8:2-3 NRSV, italics added)

To claim to know *God* and simultaneously to reject the *good* is a blatant contradiction—verbal and existential. There is no knowledge of God without ethical commitment.

Furthermore, Hosea makes it crystal clear that such ethically transformative knowledge of God is far more important to God than any religious ritual—including even sacrifices that God himself had instituted. Hosea 6:6 is justly famous as a succinct summary of the priorities of God himself.

> For I desire steadfast love and not sacrifice,
> > the knowledge of God rather than burnt offerings.
> (Hos 6:6 NRSV)

Almost certainly there is an echo here of the ancient words of Samuel to disobedient Saul.

Does the LORD delight in burnt offerings and sacrifices
as much as in obeying the voice of the LORD?
To obey is better than sacrifice,
and to heed is better than the fat of rams. (1 Sam 15:22)

And they are quoted in turn, twice and with emphatic approval, by Jesus in his critique of his own contemporaries for their religious zeal that was heedless of the ethical priorities of God himself (Mt 9:13; 12:7).

Not surprisingly, then, as we read on in Hosea, this demand for radical ethical change—as definitive of what it means to know God through repentance—comes again and again. Two examples suffice:

Sow for yourselves righteousness,
reap the fruit of unfailing love,
and break up your unplowed ground;
for it is time to seek the LORD,
until he comes
and showers righteousness on you. (Hos 10:12)

But you must return to your God;
maintain love and justice,
and wait for your God always. (Hos 12:6)

Notice the key ethical words, so typical not only of Hosea, but of the ethical teaching of the whole Old Testament: righteousness, faithfulness (hesed, "unfailing love" or "mercy"), love and justice. These are the qualities of life that God requires of those who would claim to know him, as we saw in our reflections on Jeremiah 9:23-24. And these will be the gift of God, the bridegroom, to his bride in the restored marriage to which we will turn in a moment.

But to conclude this section, Hosea reminds us that fine words are not enough. God seeks specific repentance over named sins, based on clear-eyed recognition and wholehearted renunciation of them. We have not begun to know God without that first step on the journey. And God makes clear that his priority is ethics over religion. Even those elements of religious practice that have biblical foundations are no substitute for practical obedience. And such biblical obedience is never merely a matter of private piety, but a commitment to social justice and compassion that mirrors the biblically revealed character of God.

We cannot claim to know God while colluding in injustice, cruelty and the idolizing of money, sex and power. By these standards, what might Hosea have to say to the deeply compromised Christianity of the western world?

The restoration that God promises. So, finally, we turn back to that marriage of Hosea and the profound message of love, betrayal and restoration that it embodied. In a sense Hosea 1—3 anticipates and summarizes the message of the rest of the book, and that is why we needed to explore some of the relevant sections from the later chapters before coming back to hear again the words of ultimate promise that are contained in Hosea 2.

And what wonderful words they are.

Take a moment to read again Hosea 2:2-13. It is a searing indictment of Israel, portrayed as an unfaithful, ungrateful and forgetful wife. The imagery is of divorce (Hos 2:2), shame (Hos 2:3), rejection (Hos 2:4), promiscuity (Hos 2:5), ingratitude (Hos 2:8) and punishment (Hos 2:10-13).

"Therefore," begins Hosea 2:14. Therefore what? Surely all prophetic precedent would lead us to expect a word of deserved judgment—the sentence ("guilty"), and the verdict ("destruction"). But the eyes of the prophet scan far beyond that inevitability. The reality of God's judgment on Israel lay in the immediate future and would be fulfilled in Hosea's own lifetime. But God's purposes in and through Israel went far beyond the present sinful generation. Accordingly, the prophet's vision sees far beyond the coming judgment to a future filled with hope, restoration and blessing. And to capture it for our imagination, he continues with the rich metaphor of love and marriage.

> Therefore, I will now allure her,
>> and bring her into the wilderness,
>> and speak tenderly to her.
> From there I will give her her vineyards,
>> and make the Valley of Achor a door of hope.
> There she shall respond as in the days of her youth,
>> as at the time when she came out of the land of Egypt.
> On that day, says the LORD, you will call me, "My husband," and no longer will you call me, "My Baal." For I will remove the names of the Baals from her mouth, and they shall be mentioned by name no more. I will make for you a covenant on that day with the wild animals, the birds of the air, and the creeping things of the ground; and I will abolish the bow, the sword, and war from the land; and I will make you lie down in safety. And I will take you for my wife forever; I will take you for my wife in righteousness and in justice, in steadfast love, and in mercy. I will take you for my wife in faithfulness; and you shall know the LORD. (Hos 2:14-20 NRSV)

We cannot dwell on each of the kaleidoscope images in this sparkling passage, but merely spin through them. It starts with the wooing, or alluring, by the heavenly suitor, longing to win back the love of his estranged wife. It moves on through a replay of the exodus, wilderness and conquest story, portrayed as a second honeymoon. It graphically insists on the daring sexual imagery of Yahweh as husband and Israel as wife, and uses that to exclude not only the blight of Israel's promiscuous attraction to the sexually degraded Baal worship, but even the names of the Baals themselves. It lifts our imagination even further with a vision of ecological renewal and international peace. Finally it invites us to witness the betrothal party, at which in Israelite custom gifts would be offered to the family of the bride. What gifts will the bridegroom bring to this marriage? Nothing less than the precious treasure of his own divine character, the fivefold list that summarizes the covenant identity of Yahweh himself: righteousness and justice, committed love and compassion, and trustworthiness. And these things will seal the marriage eternally.

But if these are the gifts that God brings to the marriage, what is expected of the bride? Nothing other than the same qualities reflected in her own life and relationships. The strongly ethical nature of God's character is the source of the ethical core of covenant relationship between God and his people.

And once again, we find that this is precisely what is meant by knowing God. For the climax of the whole scene is the final phrase of Hosea 2:20, *"and you shall know the Lord."* Everything else in the whole dynamic sequence, from wooing to wedding, is for that purpose and is summed up in that experience.

The climactic position of this phrase in Hosea 2:20 mirrors the equally climactic position of the end of Hosea 2:13 (which in turn echoes Hos 2:8). The whole sequence of Israel's fickleness and failure could be summed up in two words in Hebrew: *"Me she forgot."* Israel's covenant-breaking betrayal of Yahweh, their moral, social, political and spiritual breakdown, could all be attributed to this profound accusation—they had forgotten Yahweh. Now we have seen already that to say Israel "did not know Yahweh" does not imply they had lost all awareness of God by that name. So also, to say that Israel had "forgotten Yahweh" did not mean that they suffered collective amnesia about the name itself. To forget someone is relational, not just cognitive. If one person says of another, "You've forgotten me," it means that the other person has lost any sense of commitment or obligation; the shared history no longer means anything; the love has died; the relationship holds no further personal investment. So it was between Israel and God, in Hosea's accusation.

From that devastating word at the end of Hosea 2:13, then, to the exhilarating promise in Hosea 2:20, we have leapt a mighty chasm, spanned only by the breathtaking love and grace of God. We have been transported from betrayal, adultery and marital breakdown (as Hosea's metaphor for Israel's sin, in which is mirrored our own), to covenant intimacy, ethical integrity and eternal security.

CONCLUSION

Of course, we understand that Hosea is describing a future that lies as yet beyond us—in its ultimate fulfillment. His language and concepts here were further developed by Jeremiah, who called the restoration of Israel what it truly would be—a new covenant (Jer 31:31-34). The New Testament teaches us that we already have the inauguration of this new covenant in the crucified and risen Christ, and the bride of Christ awaits the bridegroom's return to consummate the relationship in the kind of perfection that Hosea and other prophets glimpsed and stammered to express.

But although these are future realities to which we look forward with eager anticipation, they are vitally relevant to how we live now. For we are called to know God here and now. And in this chapter we have explored Hosea's profound insights into what that means. God longs to be known by us, as savior, as father, as husband. We run terrible risks of forfeiting the knowledge of God when we refuse to recognize his gifts, fail to live by his standards, and neglect the teaching of his words and ways. But God in his relentlessly persistent love longs to bring us to true repentance and joyful restoration. There is, Hosea would say, a sweetness greater than even the most loving human marriage when we return to the love that sought us and bought us, woos us and wins us.

8

Knowing God in
Expectation of His Victory

Of all the places you might think of looking for teaching on Gog and Magog, a book on "Knowing God," is probably not one of them. They feature in plenty of "end-times" pot-boilers—books purporting to give us a "prophetic" timetable for the end of the world as we know it, in Armageddon almanacs, and the like. But what have Gog and Magog got to do with knowing God? It may come as a surprise to hear that, when you study the text of Ezekiel 38—39 carefully, knowing God is the emphatic and repeated point of the whole prophecy. Not that you'd have guessed that from the way they are used (and abused) in much popular futuristic scaremongering.[1]

In our survey of biblical texts so far in this book we have observed that knowing God can indeed be an intensely personal experience— through prayer, for example, and certainly through repentance. But we have also seen that God is known in action—both his action and our own. We know God through the great things he has done and continues to do, and we know him by responding in practical imitation of his commitment to compassion and justice. In this chapter we

---

[1] I have tried to provide a more balanced survey of these chapters in *The Message of Ezekiel,* The Bible Speaks Today (Downers Grove, Ill.: InterVarsity Press, 2001).

move to a more future-orientated knowing of God.

One of the great phrases of Ezekiel is in the future tense: "Then you will know" or "then they will know" usually followed by "that I am the LORD," or some other truth about who God is or what he has done. This phrase occurs more than eighty times in his book, so much so that it is like a kind of signature tune. Ezekiel is consumed by a passionate desire that people should come to know God for who God really is. Or to be more accurate, God is the one who passionately wills to be known—by his people and by the entire world—and Ezekiel is his mouthpiece. If any book of the Bible could be subtitled *Knowing God,* it would be the book of Ezekiel.

We could dip into it almost anywhere and find relevant texts for our theme in this book, but I have chosen the two chapters about Gog and Magog, Ezekiel 38—39, not only because they are so much misused and misunderstood, but also because they make crucial statements about the knowledge of God in relation to God's future victory over his enemies and protection of his people, and these need to be brought into close connection with New Testament teaching on those same themes. We need to know the God whom, according to these chapters, all nations will one day come to know in a shattering encounter with his reality. Before reading the chapters fully, take a moment to read the following key verses within them, so that you can see how prominent this theme is as a thread running through both chapters and bringing them to a grand climax: Ezekiel 38:16, 23; 39:6-7; 21-23, 27-29.

GOG AND MAGOG—THE MOVIE

The story in double outline. It would help to pause and read through Ezekiel 38—39 at this point, but just before you do, it is worth knowing in advance that each chapter is like a panel on which the same story is told, with slight variations and additions of detail. Basically, we have one story told twice over, rather like a cartoon movie. I use the word "cartoon" because the language, imagery and pictures that are brought before the eyes of our imagination in these chapters are deliberately grotesque and horrific. There is a "monster" quality about the whole scenario, and we need to take this form of writing into account before we attempt to interpret these chapters with wooden literalism.

The story can be fairly simply told.

Some mysterious character by the name of Gog, from the land of Magog, chief prince of Meshech and Tubal, will lead an alliance of other nations from the north to attack Israel. At the time (which is in some unspecified future) Israel will be living peacefully in her own land, without any military defenses, and all unsuspecting of the plot being hatched against her. However, behind the scenes it is actually Yahweh who will be controlling events so that this hostile alliance of nations, far from carrying off plunder as they expected, will be massively defeated and slain by Yahweh himself, with accompanying cosmic phenomena (earthquake, plague, blood, fire, hail and brimstone). These enemy armies will be so big that, after their climactic defeat and destruction, it will take Israel seven months to bury the dead, during which time the scavenging birds and beasts will eat their fill. And the captured weapons of war will be so many that they will provide firewood for seven years. The end result will be that both Israel and all the nations will know conclusively that Yahweh is God and that the historical events of exile and restoration were all his doing. Thus, Yahweh's greatness, holiness and glory will finally be revealed and fully vindicated in the whole earth and to all nations—including his enemies.

A closer look. With that synopsis in mind, we can discern seven sections in the double account of the visionary attack and defeat. A brief run through these paragraphs will add some local (and rather lurid) color to the outlines.

1. *Ezekiel 38:3-9.* A grand alliance of "many nations" musters to attack and invade the people of God. But already God's sovereignty can be seen at work behind all the human planning: "I will turn you around . . . and bring you out" (Ezek 38:4). God is in charge even as implacable enemies plot their evil. The reader is given the hint that we are talking about some unspecified future, "after many days . . . in future years" (Ezek 38:8), not a tight historical prediction.

2. *Ezekiel 38:10-13.* The diabolical evil of Gog's intentions is now made clear. This is not a normal war between equally armed enemies, but a devastating attack upon "'a peaceful and unsuspecting people—all of them living without walls and without gates and bars" (Ezek 38:11)—i.e., a demilitarized community. This was certainly not the condition of the kingdoms of Israel and Judah before the exile, with their fortified cities and armies. Nor, thanks to Nehemiah, was it the condition of Judah after the exile. And equally certainly it could not by any stretch of imagination describe the modern state of Israel today, which is so often unhesitatingly read into this chapter by commentators convinced that these chapters describe some future attack on that country.

3. *Ezekiel 38:14-16.* The invaders arrive in overwhelming numbers and force. But, just as previous prophets had said about previous invaders, the one who leads them is none other than Yahweh himself. But whereas in the past the purpose of God bringing enemies against Israel was to punish the Israelites, on this occasion it will be to destroy the enemies themselves, "so that the nations may know me when I show myself holy through you before their eyes" (Ezek 38:16). As with Pharaoh (Ex 9:16), and Cyrus (Is 45:5-6), God su-

pervises human plans and actions in such a way that in the end it is God's own name and glory that are made known in the world.

4. Ezekiel 38:17-23. The first main panel of the narrative in Ezekiel 38 closes with the good news for Israel that Yahweh himself will intervene to defend his otherwise defenseless people. Gog and all his hordes will meet more than their match when they face the "hot anger" of Yahweh. Not only is the future attack and defeat of Gog and his forces entirely under God's *control*, it was also within God's prophetic *foresight*. God's defenseless people may be taken by surprise, but God himself would not be. The fact that he warns his people of this impending attack means that, even if they may not know when it will actually happen, God himself has it covered.

The highly symbolic language that Ezekiel uses to describe how Yahweh will destroy these enemies of his people in Ezekiel 38:19-22 shows that we are not reading an account of history in advance, but a rhetorical vision of God in action. So there will be earthquake, environmental disaster, mountains trembling and crumbling, sword, plague, bloodshed, hail, fire and brimstone. A list like this immediately brings up memories of the flood, Sodom and Gomorrah, and the plagues of Egypt. We are being assured that, in every way possible, God will defeat and destroy his enemies. And the effect, we are reminded once again, will be the universal extension of the knowledge of God (Ezekiel 38:23).

5. Ezekiel 39:1-16. As we begin Ezekiel 39, we are taken back to the beginning of the story, and we are reminded that everything is being choreographed by God himself. We are not told how Yahweh will disarm and defeat this enemy—but it is his direct action alone. This is not some great battle with the armies of Israel—they have none. Ezekiel uses seven different words for all the captured armor and weapons, says that this will keep Israel in firewood for seven years, and that the slaughter will be so great that it will take seven months to bury the dead. This triple use of seven is also symbolic and helps us see that this is not a literal expectation but a figurative assurance of the climactic defeat of God's enemies.

6. *Ezekiel 39:17-20.* Ezekiel knew how to shock his listeners and readers. Here he creates a grotesque mental picture with graphic detail, like some wild cartoon. Even if all the corpses of the defeated enemy were to be buried, the length of time it would take would give ample freedom to the scavenging birds and animals. Such is always the horrible reality of war in any age. But Ezekiel imagines these animals actually being invited as if to a sacrificial banquet. When we confront such a grisly image we must first of all recognize that this is deliberately exaggerated and caricatured language, not a literal prediction. And then secondly we must be aware that such horrifying imagery conveys a horrifying reality: those who utterly and implacably remain enemies of God and his people, without repentance, will ultimately face utter destruction. Jesus' images of worms and smoldering fire may be more familiar, but are no less devastating in their effect. Knowing God is a serious matter.

7. *Ezekiel 39:21-29.* With the armies of Gog comprehensively defeated, devoured and buried, there is nothing more to say about them. They disappear from the story as suddenly as they had entered it. But the learning goes on. And in this final section the theme of knowing God comes to a double climax. We are told what the nations will learn, and what Israel, as God's people will learn—and indeed what they need to learn even now before these things come to pass. We shall return to these lessons shortly.

Who or what is Gog? But first it is probably worth giving just some thought to the question that immediately arises in people's mind at this point—who or what is this mysterious "Gog of the land of Magog"? Here is an extract from some comments I made on this in the Bible Speaks Today *Message of Ezekiel*.

> The honest answer is that nobody really knows, but not for want of trying. Certainly, there is no such person known within the rest of Old Testament history. . . . Probably Daniel 11:40-45 has been influenced by the story of Gog. . . . Early Christian eschatology also made use of Ezekiel's imagery to portray the great conflict between the forces of evil, both human and satanic, and the reign of God and Christ. Revelation 19:11-20:15 envisages a mighty attack by the massed forces of evil, led by Satan, but including "Gog and Magog" (20:8), which is comprehensively defeated.[2]

As the centuries of the Christian era passed, different generations have identified Gog with whatever fearsome foe of the day seemed to fit, or needed to be placed under the comforting prospect of God's terrible destruction. Augustine, for example, saw Gog in the faces of the terrible onslaughts of the Goths upon the Roman Empire, which seemed to signal the end of Christian civilization as then known. Luther identified Gog and Magog with the dreaded Turks of his day (with some geographical correspondence at least in his favor). In the twentieth century, a popular and influential brand of Christian fundamentalism confidently identified Gog and Magog with the communist Soviet empire. "Rosh" (the Hebrew word meaning "head" and translated as *chief prince* in the NIV, Ezek 38:2), was obviously Russia; *Meshech* must therefore be Moscow, and *Tubal* none other than Tobolsk. On this flimsiest of word association (which has no etymological credibility whatever), the Christian world was warned of an impend-

---

[2]Ibid., p. 324.

ing invasion of the land of the modern state of Israel by the armies of the Soviet empire to the north, which would spark off the final great battle of Armageddon, and other events already plotted on a particular millennialist timechart. God, as well as Gog, had his marching orders. Those who were skeptical about the whole scenario were accused of not being prepared to take the Bible literally—to which a sufficient reply seemed to be that, if the foe from the north was to be literally equated with a Russian army invading modern Israel, then presumably we should expect them to be riding horses and fighting with bows and arrows. Even literalists have problems with consistency. And, we might add, literalism of this sort is not noted for its humility either. The collapse of the Soviet empire without a Russian soldier setting foot on the soil of Israel, let alone hordes of them being buried there, has not been marked by a chorus of the prophets of Armageddon-in-our-time saying, "Thanks for all the money we made out of the books making that prediction, but actually, sorry, we seem to have got it wrong."

My main problem with this kind of literalistic application of Ezekiel's vision to confident "end-times" predictions is that it ends up totally distracting the consumers of the pulp-industry that produces them from the clear and intentional message that Ezekiel wanted us to hear. The primary and repeated point of the double chapter narrative is that Yahweh will be fully, finally and victoriously revealed in his true identity and in the justice of his ways. That revelation will be both to his people and to all nations on earth.

The defeat of God's enemies and the protection of God's people will lead both of them to *know God*. Not, we might add, to *know Gog*. For whoever, or whatever Gog may be, has been, or will be, his only reason for existence is that God will display his own glory through him. To spend our time in fascinated obsession speculating about the identity of Gog is to miss the whole point. *It doesn't matter who Gog is. It matters eternally who God is.* It seems tragically ironic that so many people, ancient and modern, devote endless energy trying to know who the legendary Gog might be, when the infinitely more important task is to know who the living God actually is.

Having said this, however, it seems to me, to quote once more from *The Message of Ezekiel,* that

> we can see two levels of fulfilment. On the one hand, the symbolism speaks of an ever present reality, namely human and satanic opposition to God and his people. History is littered with "Gogs"—those who have thought they would eradicate the people of God. They have not triumphed so far, and this vision affirms that they never will. On the other hand, the extension and application of Ezekiel's vision by John in Revelation leads us to anticipate that the battle between God and his enemies will ultimately come to a climactic finale in which all the forces of Satan and those who have allied with him will be defeated by the power of Christ and then destroyed forever.[3] The defeat and destruction of Gog thus offers us prophetic assurance of the ultimate defeat and destruction of all that opposes God and endangers his people.[4]

So then, rather than any single identification, "Gog" represents all those who oppose God, attack his people and seek to destroy them— of whom there have been many and doubtless many more to come. But these chapters give rock-solid assurance to God's people that God

---

[3]In this double application (to continuing historical enemies of God's people, and to a climactic eschatological defeat of the ultimate enemy of God and his people), our interpretation is similar to that adopted by many in respect of the New Testament figure of "antichrist."
[4]Wright, *Message of Ezekiel,* p. 326.

will ultimately defeat all such enemies. Here in Ezekiel, as in the book of Revelation, this is a necessary precursor to what follows. In Ezekiel 40—48 we have the picture of God once again dwelling in the midst of his people in the rebuilt temple. Such an idyllic picture needed the assurance that what had happened once would never happen again—namely an attack on God's city, people and temple. No, Ezekiel 38—39 declare in advance, that will never happen because those who would want to do that will have been eradicated. Similarly, in Revelation 21—22 we have the corresponding picture, consciously drawing from Ezekiel, of the dwelling place of God in the midst of the redeemed humanity in the new creation. And the eternal security of that state of affairs is guaranteed, because, just as Ezekiel 38—39 eliminates all that could threaten the restored Israel of God, so the preceding chapters of Revelation have described the ultimate purging of all that is satanic, wicked and anti-God from God's new creation.

> Just as the picture of comprehensive destruction of evil in Ezekiel 38—39 ushers in the prospect of Yahweh dwelling with Israel reconstituted in their land and worshipping him in the perfection of his restored sanctuary (Ezek. 40—48), so the defeat of Satan in Revelation 19—20 ushers in the great vision of God dwelling with his people drawn from all nations in a new creation, worshipping the Lamb in the perfection of his presence that will need no temple (Rev. 21—22).[5]

WHAT GOG AND THE NATIONS WILL KNOW

You will advance against my people Israel like a cloud that covers the land. In days to come, O Gog, I will bring you against

---

[5]Ibid.

my land, so that the nations may know me when I show myself
holy through you before their eyes. (Ezek 38:16, italics added)

And so I will show my *greatness* and my *holiness,* and I will make
myself known in the sight of many nations. Then they will
know that I am the LORD. (Ezek 38:23, italics added)

I will display my *glory* among the nations, and all the nations
will see the punishment I inflict and the hand I lay upon them.
(Ezek 39:21, italics added)

The italicized words pinpoint the message for us. What the world
will come to know, by one means or another, is the holiness, the
greatness and the glory of Yahweh, the only living God.

- *His holiness,* because he is utterly different from all other claimants
  to deity. He is above and beyond us and the universe, in his being,
  his moral character, and in his ways and actions.

- *His greatness,* because he is immeasurable and incomparable (Is
  40). If the greatest things we can contemplate (the oceans, the
  mountains, the heavens) are tiny in comparison, how infinitely
  great must their Creator and sustainer be?

- *His glory,* because he is the only God with reality, substance,
  "weight" (as the word literally means). His glory includes the vast
  fullness of the whole earth (Is 6), and yet transcends the heavens,
  for he has set his glory above the clouds.

Eventually the whole human race will know the truth about their
Creator, in contrast to all the idolatries that we run after, which are
unholy and dirty, pathetically insignificant, and futile in their empti-
ness. This is an awesome prospect, and yet it is also a hope-filled one.

As we seek to live as the people of God in the midst of a hostile world (just as the Israel of Ezekiel's vision and indeed the Israelites of Ezekiel's ministry in exile), we are surrounded by peoples and their gods that give no allegiance to the God we know and love. In mission, we seek to engage with such people. Sometimes we find ourselves mocked by the gods of our culture: the idols of the rich and powerful in society; the symbols of affluence, arrogance and greed; the overwhelming machinery of economic and military domination; the threats and rivalry of some other faiths; the cynicism and pomposity of the media; the dazzling enticement of the prizes our society holds out for success or celebrity, etc. At times we and the churches we serve can feel weak, marginal, exposed, vulnerable to attack, defenseless against the powerful hostilities ranged against us. And in some parts of the world, of course, the hostility of the world against the church takes a literally violent form, and many of our sisters and brothers in Christ experience physical threats and assault, social disadvantage, immense psychological and spiritual pressures, imprisonment, torture and death. The language of Gog is not out of place in such circumstances.

But the Bible lifts up our eyes, our heads and our hearts. There will come a day, promises our Lord God, when the gods of the nations will be exposed for the empty sham that they really are, and when all the nations themselves will know who the only true and living God is, in all his holiness, greatness and glory. If this takes place within the context of searing judgment, as the narrative of the destruction of the armies of Gog and his allies portrays, it will nevertheless constitute unmistakable, undeniable and unavoidable knowledge of the living God.

Such a prospect, of course, gives us no joy, for it gives God no joy. This same prophet declares that God takes no pleasure in the death of the wicked, but rather that he should turn from his wickedness and live. But it does give us a perspective, an expectation and a hope. The wicked will not defy God forever. The false gods will not deceive the nations forever. As in the book of Revelation, the ultimate exposure and destruction of the enemies of God is an unavoidable corollary of the ultimate security of his people and redemption of his creation.

WHAT GOD'S PEOPLE WILL KNOW

These chapters were addressed originally to the exiles of Israel in Babylon, in the midst of precisely one of the Gogs that had tried to destroy their nation, their city, their temple and their God. So there is huge implicit encouragement in the message contained here. When Ezekiel says that Israel "will know" something, it also implies that the learning should start here and now. We should begin now to know God in ways that anticipate the full knowledge of God that will come only when these great events reach their final fulfillment and are consigned to the old order that will forever be past.

So what was Israel to know, and what are we to know as we sit with them?

That all God's judgment was righteous.

> From that day forward the house of Israel will know that I am the LORD their God. And the nations will know that the people of Israel went into exile for their sin, because they were unfaithful to me. So I hid my face from them and handed them over to their enemies, and they all fell by the sword. I dealt with them according to their uncleanness and their offenses, and I hid my face from them. (Ezek 39:22-24)

Israel (and the nations) will come to know that there was nothing undeserved, unfair or excessive in what God had done. It was a key element of Israel's faith from the beginning that Yahweh the God of Israel was in his own self and character the definitive standard of justice. "Will not the Judge of all the earth do right?" asks Abraham (Gen 18:25). But Israel had often complained that it did not seem so, and Ezekiel particularly wrestled with people who were obsessed with that perverse perception of the ways of God. Nevertheless the day will come, Ezekiel insists through the graphic message of these two chapters, when everybody will know (whether part of God's covenant people or not), that God's punitive actions were utterly appropriate. He simply could not allow sin to go unpunished forever. He could no longer let his name be treated as "profane." He had acted out of the perfect justice of his own character.

Such knowledge of God, while it will be perfected in the future, ought to grasp us here and now in our consciousness. Yes, we know that in Christ we are spared the condemnation we deserve (Rom 8). Such is the glorious good news of the gospel. But let us always have in mind, with perennial gratitude, that it is only by the grace of God that we stand upright in that knowledge. Only because of the blood of Christ will it be true that the judgment that will ultimately fall on those who remain unrepentant enemies of God in their persistent wickedness will not fall on us.

That God's restoring grace is personal and unbelievably generous.

> Then they will know that I am the LORD their God, for though I sent them into exile among the nations, I will gather them to their own land, not leaving any behind. I will no longer hide my face from them, for I will pour out my Spirit on the house of Israel, declares the Sovereign LORD. (Ezek 39:28-29)

These words were spoken to people who had experienced precisely the opposite in their own history. They had known God turning his face away in grief and anger at their sin (Ezek 39:23). But now they will know the restoration of Aaronic blessing—God's face turned toward them in personal grace. The frown of judgment is replaced by the smile of love. They had known God pouring out his anger (Ezek 7:8; 9:8; 20:8, etc.), but now they will know the pouring out of his Spirit.

CONCLUSION

"Consider therefore the kindness and sternness of God," says Paul, in Romans 11:22. This chapter has opened our eyes to both. They go inseparably together. For the grace and kindness with which God will protect his people is an intrinsic part of the severity with which he will oppose and defeat all who seek to destroy them. Knowing God must therefore take the fullest account of the scope of these searing chapters—for that is their express purpose: "then they will know." The challenge to us is to ensure that we ourselves know God in his saving grace, and that we urgently seek to bring others to know him, others who as yet are strangers to his covenant mercy and in danger of being counted finally among his enemies.

9

Knowing God Through
Trusting in His Sovereignty

I first preached a sermon on Psalm 46, combined with Habakkuk, on Wednesday, January 16, 1991, at the weekly worship service at All Nations Christian College. That was the day the coalition forces, led by the USA, invaded Iraq in defense of Kuwait in the first Gulf War against Saddam Hussein. It was a harder message to prepare than any I had preached for a long time. There was a palpable fear among many people that this conflict could lead to a Third World War, if Israel and then Russia were drawn into it. I shared that fear, but I remember many other mixed emotions as well, that I recorded in my notes.

I felt angry at the human madness that, on the western side of the Red Sea millions of poverty stricken people in Ethiopia were facing starvation, while on the eastern side of it, billions of dollars were feeding the machinery of war.

I felt confusion and despair at why this war was deemed necessary, what the real motivation for it was, why we had to be involved in it— and sick of the moral hypocrisy that surrounded it.

I felt some biblical *déjà vu*, seeing maps on the TV news bulletins that you normally associate only with the pages at the back of your Bible, maps which were now the scene of a modern replay of some biblical stories. There on the TV was what we call "Mesopotamia," or in biblical scholarship, "the Ancient Near East." It was the land of the tower of Babel, of Ur of the Chaldees and Abraham's migration. It was the land of Nineveh and Jonah, of Nebuchadnezzar and Babylon. And it was where the Bible locates the Garden of Eden. How short is human history! How small is human geography!

Most of all, as the father of two sons who were seventeen and eighteen at the time—the same age as some who would be fighting in yet another war—I felt the horror of yet more shattered families with grieving mothers, wives, orphans.

But what could I preach? What *can* you preach in the face of the brutal realities of war?

At All Nations in 1991, I was preaching to people who were training for crosscultural mission. Single men and women, married folk with families, all heading into difficult situations, some into parts of the world that are endemically wracked with conflict and war. I have visited some of them in such locations since then, in Afghanistan for example, and most recently in Chad, where I preached from Psalm 46 and Habakkuk yet again, to people living in daily preparedness for an escalation of the internecine war in that land.

Psalm 46 and the prophecy of Habakkuk speak powerfully into times of war and international chaos—precisely because they speak from within such realities. Psalm 46 comes from some unspecified time of national emergency, when it seemed that the earth itself was dissolving in the maelstrom of violence and confusion being unleashed around the people of God.

What sort of song was a hymn-writer supposed to produce in the midst of such extreme danger?

Habakkuk lived in the dark days that preceded the Babylonian invasion, which brought about the destruction of Jerusalem and the exile of the people. The horror of anticipating those events was very real, since nobody in those days had any illusions about the mind-numbing brutality of what happened when cities were besieged and finally captured, when whole populations were decimated and enslaved.

What was a prophet supposed to think and preach in such days?

And we live now in a world that seems to become more dangerous and terrifying by the week. At the time of writing this, more than a thousand people a month are being slaughtered in Iraq, and Lebanon is in ruins. Nobody is counting the numbers killed in less publicized conflicts in some parts of Africa. The so-called "War on Terror" makes us all afraid, while violence often seems only just below the surface of some of the most sophisticated European cities, with its roots in ethnic and religious divisions and the fruit of ancient colonial injustices and contemporary economic inequalities.

What is a preacher supposed to hear from God's Word and declare through the spoken or written word for such a time?

And what does it mean to know God in such times? Both Psalm 46 and Habakkuk speak about knowing God. In fact the following two texts seemed essential to include in any book about the knowledge of God, and also seemed to fit together well as the foundation for this final chapter.

Be still, and know that I am God;
    I will be exalted among the nations,
    I will be exalted in the earth. (Ps 46:10)

For the earth will be filled with the knowledge of the glory of
        the LORD,
    as the waters cover the sea. (Hab 2:14)

The psalmist and the prophet help us to remind ourselves of some of the central truths about our God, so that in knowing them (and knowing him), we may put our trust in God even in the extreme turbulence that surrounds us. And then, as we exercise that trust and grow in that knowledge, how are we to go on living? Let us then remember the God we know, and then choose to live as those who know God.

TRUSTING THE GOD WE KNOW

God remains in control of the world. The lesson that Ezekiel taught us in the last chapter was well known to the song-writers of Israel. The world is not run by its human rulers, but by the living God. He is the God of all creation and equally Lord of all history. The psalmist looks at the earth, the sea and the mountains, and imagines all of them in turbulence—roaring, quaking, surging (Ps 46:2-3). But if you know who created them, you need not live in fear of even such frightening phenomena. He then extends the metaphor to the world of nations, similarly in turmoil. But if you know who is actually in charge, then behind all the human plotting and scheming, you are invited to see the hand of the Lord at work.

> Nations are in uproar, kingdoms fall;
>> *he* lifts his voice, the earth melts.
> The LORD Almighty is with us;
>> the God of Jacob is our fortress.
> Come and see *the works of the* LORD,
>> the desolations *he* has brought on the earth.
> (Ps 46:6-8, italics added)

Habakkuk was baffled and frightened by the national and international events of his day. His own nation seemed a chaotic mess of violence, conflict, breakdown of law and order, and absence of justice.

He puts this problem to God in Habakkuk 1:2-4. And he gets an answer that seems even more puzzling. To solve the problem of his own sinful people, God is raising up a larger, and apparently even more sinful, nation to act as the agent of his judgment upon them—the Babylonians. This is not just an accident of history. It is the deliberate work of God.

> Look at the nations and watch—and be utterly amazed. For *I am going to do something* in your days that you would not believe, even if you were told. *I am raising up* the Babylonians, that ruthless and impetuous people, who sweep across the whole earth to seize dwelling places not their own. (Hab 1:5-6)

This was not a new message of course. Isaiah had said the same thing a century before about the Assyrians, whom God had lifted up like a stick to beat Israel with (Is 7:18-20; 10:5-19). But it is not a message that is easy to hear and believe in the present. Looking back, we can easily talk with all the wisdom of theological hindsight about how God has been sovereign over the march of history. But when the world is falling apart around you, it is not such an obvious stance to adopt or truth to believe. And yet that is when it is even more vital that we *do* remember this truth.

When the axe actually did fall and Nebuchadnezzar finally attacked and destroyed Jerusalem and carried the bulk of the population of Judah off into two generations of demeaning exile, Jeremiah wrote a letter to the exiles in which he helped them to see things from this perspective.

At the human level, they were the people whom "Nebuchadnezzar had carried into exile from Jerusalem to Babylon" (Jer 29:1). That is what you would have seen, with human eyes, at the ground level of human history: an invasion; a siege; suffering and death; defeat; capture; exile. And who was responsible? Nebuchadnezzar and his armies. But at the level of prophetic insight there was another hand involved. Jeremiah's letter begins with that higher perspective:

> This is what the LORD Almighty, the God of Israel, says to all those *I carried into exile* from Jerusalem to Babylon. (Jer 29:4, italics added)

For, as God had already told them years before, when Jeremiah had broken into an international Middle East diplomatic conference being held in Jerusalem, Nebuchadnezzar was merely a tool in the hands of the sovereign God of Israel.

> Give them a message for their masters and say, "This is what the LORD Almighty, the God of Israel, says: 'Tell this to your masters: With my great power and outstretched arm I made the earth and its people and the animals that are on it, and I give it to anyone I please. Now I will hand all your countries over to *my servant Nebuchadnezzar* king of Babylon; I will make even the wild animals subject to him. All nations will serve him and his son and his grandson until the time for his land comes; then many nations and great kings will subjugate him.' " (Jer 27:4-7, italics added)

God remained in control right through the darkest days of Israel's Old Testament history. In fact, the surprising thing is that the Israelites held on to this affirmation when everything seemed to deny it. From a Babylonian perspective the matter was much simpler: the gods of Babylon had defeated the god of Israel. Yahweh was no better or stronger than the other gods of the pathetic little nations that had been trampled by the armies of the new empire. But Israel's faith was at its most amazing when, in such times, the worst and weakest

times, they could still affirm, "Our God reigns." The language of
Psalm 47 already flavors the confidence of Psalm 46. The assurance
that Habakkuk draws from his knowledge of God's sovereignty in Israel's past sustains his hope in the fearful prospect of the present and
future (Hab 3).

Knowing God, then, means knowing the God who is in charge of
current affairs—and trusting him when the world goes mad.

God works out his judgment in history. When wars happen the
issue of justice is invariably raised. Does either party in the conflict
have "right on its side"? If a country is attacked, is it justified in fighting back to defend itself? If one country attacks another, is a third
country justified in intervening to defend the weaker country
against the attacker? For many centuries, Christians have sought to
define a "just war" ethic, setting out strict criteria (which are almost
impossible to satisfy in most conflicts, especially as the momentum
and brutality of war gather pace), by which a war might be deemed
just, so that those waging it may salvage some sense of their actions
in the war being "justified." These are issues that Christians rightly
struggle with and there are agonies of conscience down whatever
road is followed.

From a biblical perspective, we have to affirm that human justice
ultimately depends upon and flows from the justice of God. So any
justice that is claimed by or for a country engaged in warfare can only
be evaluated, from a Christian point of view, in relation to the judgment or justice of God within history. But that too is a far from easy
task. There is no doubt, biblically, that God "reserves the right," so to
speak, to use any nation as the agent of his judgment or justice on
any other nation. That is what he did in using the Israelites in judgment on the wickedness of the Canaanites in the generation of the
conquest. And it is what he did many more times in judgment on the

Israelites through successive generations in which they suffered divine wrath at the hands of their enemies. So the principle is established in the Old Testament. God can use one nation as an agent of justice against another.[1]

But that doesn't make it any easier to accept, Habakkuk must have thought. Habakkuk had complained to God about the injustice that was going on in his own society (Hab 1:1-4). How much longer could God put up with it and not act? God's answer shocked him (though actually, in the light of all Israel's history to this point, it shouldn't have). God was raising up the Babylonians as the agent of his judgment upon Israel, precisely because of the wickedness Habakkuk was pointing out (Hab 1:5-11).

But how could that be fair? Surely that was even worse! Could God punish the wicked who were his own people by means of even more wicked people who were not?

> Your eyes are too pure to look on evil; you cannot tolerate wrong. Why then do you tolerate the treacherous? Why are you silent while the wicked swallow up those more righteous than themselves? (Hab 1:13)

But, yes, that was exactly what God was about to do—but it was not by any means the end of the story. Babylon's time would come.

The utterly crucial point to grasp here is that, just because God uses a nation as the agent of his judgment on another does not make that first nation more righteous than the latter. God does not rule the world by the conventions of Hollywood, nor is he restricted to using only the "good guys" to accomplish his purposes. And this applied

---

[1]For a much fuller discussion of the Old Testament's theology of God and the nations—in history and the future, see Christopher J. H. Wright, *The Mission of God* (Downers Grove, Ill.: InterVarsity Press, 2006), chap. 14.

just as much to Israel as anybody else, as Deuteronomy 9 had made devastatingly clear.

Before the conquest of Canaan, God warned Israel not to fall into a simplistic, binary, logic: "The defeat of our enemies is the result of their wickedness and our righteousness. So God is on our side against them." "Not so, says God; not remotely so" (see Deut 9:4-6). Israel was right about the wickedness of the Canaanites, for which God would indeed drive them out. But they were utterly wrong about their own righteousness. For, as the list of Israel's rebellions showed, if anybody deserved to be destroyed it was the Israelites themselves. They had only the grace of God and the intercession of Moses to thank that it had not happened long ago. So God could use wicked, judgment-deserving Israelites as the agent of his judgment on Canaan. He could just as consistently use wicked, judgment-deserving Babylonians as the agent of his judgment on Israel. The outworking of God's justice in history is not a matter of siding with the good guys against the bad guys, because the reality of human behavior and relationships is far more complex and ambiguous than Hollywood endings. The stick in the hand of God by which he uses one nation as the agent of his judgment against another may be a very bent stick indeed.

Coming back to Habakkuk, then, God moves seamlessly from the fact that he is raising up the Babylonians to judge Israel, to the fact that Babylon itself stands under his judgment for a catalog of wickedness that fills the rest of Habakkuk 2. This is very similar to Jeremiah. Having written to the exiles that Nebuchadnezzar had merely carried out the will of God in carrying off the exiles to Babylon, he puts into the next diplomatic mailbag a ferocious and sustained declaration of the judgment of God that awaits Babylon itself (Jer 50—51).

And so it must also be in our day. If we choose to believe that in some of our contemporary conflicts God may use one powerful nation (or a coalition of powerful nations) as the agent of judgment on tyrannous regimes, then this says nothing, in and of itself, about the moral righteousness of the nation or nations so used. Yet, sadly, the rhetoric of self-righteousness that tends to get wrapped around the geo-political posturing of western leaders falls into exactly that presumption.

But look at the condemnation of Babylon in Habakkuk 2. This is the nation God will use as his rod of justice. Yet its catalog of wickedness strikes me as eerily modern in it relevance to western culture. Of course these words were originally aimed at Babylon, but "Babylon," as we know, becomes a universal symbol in the Bible for human societies standing in arrogant rebellion against God—ancient and modern. Where might the prophet's words be addressed today, when he highlights the following?

- Economic imperialism and plundering greed (Hab 2:6-8)
- Profiting from unjust trading (Hab 2:9)
- Secret undermining of the stability of other nations (Hab 2:10)
- Building cities at the cost of human lives (Hab 2:12)
- Ecological destructiveness ("Lebanon" probably here stands for forests; Hab 2:17)
- Rampant national idolatry, trusting in one's own resources and products (Hab 2:18-20)

So if that is God's assessment of the nation he was using as his agent of judgment, how could we have evaluated those events by the criteria of "just war"? Not without considerable ambiguity. All we can do, with Abraham, is to ask the rhetorical question that embodies its own answer, "Will not the Judge of all the earth do right?" (Gen

18:25). And then, we recall with a shudder that the question was first asked just before the judgment of God fell upon Sodom and Gomorrah, and drove Abraham to intercession—a point to which we will return below.

Knowing God means trusting God's sovereign judgment. It does not mean knowing all the answers to the ambiguities of history, or knowing the whole script in advance. And it certainly does not mean handing out medals for righteousness for those God may choose to use as agents of his own justice in world affairs.

God will defend his people. We return to Psalm 46. This psalm is astonishingly relevant to our day, because it faces up to the two terrifying realities that seem to dominate our anxieties: on the one hand, within the natural order, the known dangers of natural disasters such as earthquakes and unknown dangers of climate change; and on the other hand, within the international order, the escalating dangers of war in so many places. Psalm 46 is for such a time as this. And it opens with a resounding assertion of God's constant protection.

> God is our refuge and strength,
>   an ever-present help in trouble. (Ps 46:1)

Psalm 46:2-3 then goes on to envisage the first kind of catastrophe (natural disaster), while Psalm 46:4-7 envisages the second (war). In both cases, says the psalm, God will defend his people.

In Psalm 46:2-3 the psalmist imagines the collapse of the natural world. The language he uses pictures a kind of "uncreation." In our contemporary world, some of the doomsday scenarios used to warn us about the long-term effects of climate change, global warming, rising sea levels, environmental catastrophe and so on, would fit the language of the psalm. It is possible he is thinking of literal earthquakes and the devastating turbulence of the sea that sometimes accompanies them. Lying along the great fault that stretches through Palestine and on down to the Great Rift Valley, the land of Israel was familiar with such things.

But it is equally likely that he is using the language also in a symbolic, or apocalyptic way (as it is used, for example, in Is 24:19-20, 54:10; Hag 2:6), in which case his affirmation of God's sovereignty recalls God's conquest of chaos in creation. The mountains may slip and slide (Ps 46:2), but the God who created them is a better place of safety than they ever were anyway.

In Psalm 46:4-7 the psalmist turns to the international scene. If, in Psalm 46:2, it was the sea that was in turmoil and the mountains that were slipping and falling, in Psalm 46:6 it is the nations that "are in uproar," and kingdoms that slip and fall (the verb "fall" is the same in both verses, for the mountains and the kingdoms). The world of nations and kingdoms seems as unstable as nature in an earthquake. Everything shifts. The earth itself, where everything seemed so unmovable, has melted into a mud-patch at the voice of God (Ps 46:6). No wonder the nations are in a skid.

Where then is security to be found? Not in some mountain fortress, nor in some national security program. If mountains and men both melt before God, then the only place of safety is in God himself—which is where Psalm 46:1, 5, 7 and 10-11 place it. In Psalm 46:1, God is described in two ways: as a shelter or refuge, and as a strength or fortification. This gives both a passive and active dimension. God is a place to hide and be safe. But God is also the warrior who defends his people "at break of day" (Ps 46:5), just as he did on the night of the exodus, or in the deliverance from Sennacherib (2 Kings 19:35-36).

So the place to be when the world falls apart is in "the city of God" (Ps 46:4). For it is the only thing in this psalm that "will not fall" (Ps

46:5). This is the third time the same verb is used. Mountains—bastions of solid rock, can slip and fall (Ps 46:2). Kingdoms—even great fortified empires, slip and fall (Ps 46:6). But the city of God stands firm (Ps 46:5), for of course, as we know from the rest of the Bible, it is eternal, and stands ultimately for the new creation, where God himself dwells with his people. It is the presence of God within the city that guarantees its security against all that nature or nations can throw against it.

For who is this God in the midst?

The LORD Almighty is with us;
    the God of Jacob is our fortress. (Ps 46:7)

"The LORD Almighty" is, literally, Yahweh of Hosts—i.e., the Lord of all armies—earthly or heavenly. And "the God of Jacob" was especially remembered for his protection. Jacob himself speaks of him as "God, who answered me in the day of my distress and who has been with me wherever I have gone" (Gen 35:3). And Jacob's beautiful blessing of his two grandsons majors particularly on this note of protection:

May the God before whom my fathers
    Abraham and Isaac walked,
the God who has been my shepherd
    all my life to this day,
the Angel who has delivered me from all harm
    —may he bless these boys. (Gen 48:15-16)

Habakkuk, in similar circumstances, but knowing even beyond the perspective of the psalm that the catastrophe that was about to engulf Israel was in fact the judgment of God, nevertheless looked to God for final deliverance.

> O LORD, are you not from everlasting?
>> My God, my Holy One, we will not die.
> O LORD, you have appointed them to execute judgment;
>> O Rock, you have ordained them to punish. (Hab 1:12)

Habakkuk gathers up all his trust in God into that one ancient title: "O Rock." Israel had used this term to celebrate the delivering, protecting power of Yahweh, and the security of belonging to him, from very early on (cf. Deut 32:4, 30-31). Jesus used the same imagery in his famous parable of the wise and foolish builders, which a children's chorus has turned into song.

> Build on the rock, the rock that ever stands;
> Build on the rock, and not upon the sands.
> You need not fear the storm or the earthquake's shock;
> You're safe for evermore if you build on the rock.

This does not mean that believers will be immune from pain or suffering, that they will never face danger or death, or that believers will never get killed in times of natural catastrophe or armed attack. That was not true in Israel's day nor is it true in ours. Christians suffer and lose their lives along with others in such times. So the declaration of God's protection here is not some talisman or mantra that protects its wearer or chanter from any physical harm whatsoever. What is promised is *ultimate* security. Whatever happens, the believer's life is in God's hands. And for the believer, of course, physical death is never ultimate—death does not have the last word. The key message of this psalm, as for Habakkuk, is that God's people will survive. They will never be obliterated. The Lord knows those who are his. And those who are in Christ are in the only totally safe place. Eternally.

God will be exalted among the nations. The final verses of Psalm 46 invite us to come and see both aspects of God's power at work—over nature and over the nations. It is a curious thing that whereas many modern people look at the awesome power of nature, when it wreaks desolation, and conclude that there is no God, the biblical writers saw in such natural forces one of the great demonstrations of God's power. These things are "the works of the LORD" (Ps 46:8). But beyond the natural order, the psalmist thinks of the international order (or rather, disorder) that pervades history. And he looks forward to the end of history and anticipates the shalom of God that God alone will have created from the debris and exhaustion of all the wars of history (Ps 46:9). He sees the grim legacy of battle: broken bows, shattered spears and burnt shields—as we might scan the burnt out tanks, the shattered homes and broken lives. And out of it all, he hears the great climactic command of God himself:

"Be still, and know that I am God." (Ps 46:10)

The word does not mean "please be nice and quiet," as if addressed to people on a silent retreat, or to readers in a library. It is an abrupt and authoritative order: "Stop fighting!" "Cease fire!" It is spoken in the midst of the conflict, to bring it to a peremptory end, just as the command of Jesus, hurled at the raging wind and waves, "Peace, be still!" brought the storm to a sudden calm.

This then is the final whistle of history. The match is over. And who has finally won? Who stands alone on the battlefield? No human army. No human nation or empire claiming to have right on its side. No crooked cop posturing as the world's policeman. Only the living God will be finally exalted on that day. The world is commanded to listen up and acknowledge him for who he truly is.

So this is God's final word. He calls us to know who he is *now*, because of what he will be acknowledged to be *then*. He will be exalted. And he will be exalted in both the spheres we have been considering—"among the *nations*" and "in the *earth*." That is to say, in the international arena and in the world of nature. He is Lord of history and Lord of creation, and he will one day be exalted supremely in both.

Furthermore, if God's exaltation is to be among the nations and in the earth, it clearly means that it will be *public* and it will be *here*. This is not just some pietistic hope that God will be exalted in our hearts or up in heaven. We have already seen in earlier chapters that "knowing God" cannot be confined to private devotion or spiritual aspirations. It is something rather that God intends to fill all the earth, not just the hearts of his people.

And that is how Habakkuk gives expression to the same confident hope that brings Psalm 46 to an end.

> For the earth will be filled with the knowledge of the glory of
> the LORD,
>   as the waters cover the sea. (Hab 2:14)

This ray of light and hope comes (as in Psalm 46), in the midst of talk of God's judgment on human violence. And it echoes the promise associated with the universal and peaceful rule of God's Messiah in Isaiah 11:9.

It is rather a pity that the last line of each verse of the wonderful hymn, "God is working his purpose out," shortens Habakkuk's prophecy by omitting (doubtless to make the line fit the rhythm of the poetry), the word "knowledge," even though the original text in Isaiah has "knowledge of God," not glory. The hymn repeats:

> "When the earth shall be filled with the glory of God as the waters cover the sea."

But Habakkuk's point (and Isaiah's), is not that the *glory* of God will fill the earth some time in the future; it already does. "The whole earth is the fullness of his glory," sing the seraphim in Isaiah 6:3 (author's translation). Rather, their point is that all people will come to *know* the God whose glory they see every day simply by living in his creation. It will be the *knowledge* of God that will be universal and all-pervasive. Indeed, in this wonderful vision of our future habitation, in the new creation, the knowledge of God will be *definitive* of our new reality. It will be as impossible for there to be anywhere on earth where God is *not known,* as it is impossible for there to be a sea that is not full of water. Being covered with water is what constitutes and defines a sea. Being filled with the knowledge of God is what will constitute and define the earth in the new creation.

The God who will be universally exalted will be the God who will be universally known. This is God's mission and goal: to vindicate his own glory, to bring peace to his creation, and to be known for who he truly is by all his creatures.

LIVING AS THOSE WHO KNOW GOD

My God, my Holy One, we will not die. (Hab 1:12)

We shall not die, *we shall live.* But how? How shall we then live, we who already know this God? If we know God, then we must live as those who do. We must live in the light of what we know. And as we have seen from these two Scriptures, we know four things: that God remains in control, that God will act in just judgment within history, that God will defend his own people, and that God will finally be universally exalted. What are the matching commitments that we are called to make in response to these great affirmations?

Because we know God remains in control, we will live by faith.

Habakkuk, we have seen, was desperately baffled by the events that were unfolding in his own day. The wickedness of his own people was bad enough; the news that God intended to punish them through the Babylonians who were more wicked still, seemed even worse. Yet he remains convinced that God knows what he is doing and remains in sovereign control. So how was he to live with the tension between the present realities and the expectation of God's eventual judgment on the wickedness of Babylon too? By sustaining a firm trust in God. That was the right thing to do. That was what a person who was in a right relationship with God should do. In the midst of all the turmoil—national, international, moral and spiritual—the righteous person goes on trusting God and living by in the strength of that faith.

And so Habakkuk framed a three word sentence (in Hebrew) that came to define the very essence of the biblical gospel—for Paul, and for Christian faith ever since.

> The-righteous-person by-his-faith shall-live. (Hab 2:4, author's translation; the hyphens indicate each of the three words in Hebrew)

The contrast with the first half of the verse is with the ungodly person (or nation, since Babylon is already in view), who is puffed up with arrogance and greed, and whose life is not upright at all. Such a person has no place for God, feels no need of God, does not live by God's ways, and is certainly not right with God. The righteous person, on the other hand, such as Habakkuk was striving to be, knows that the key to life is firm trust in God.

The word "faith" here is the word that means firm, strong, committed trust. It can also mean faithfulness—that is, the kind of faithfulness to God that springs from faith in God's promises. It includes dependability, loyalty to God's covenant. Such qualities are the mark of the righteous person, and they are the way to life and living.

And it is precisely in the times of extreme danger, of natural or national catastrophe, that such faith is proved. It is when life is baffling that we affirm the sovereign reign of God *by faith,* and live accordingly. So this verse is not just defining the *starting point* of the life of a believer—through justification by faith. It is describing the *life* of faith, the habitual stance of the one who is in a right relationship with God.

Such a life of faith, of unwavering trust in God when all around seems to contradict it, is a deliberate choice and calls for constant renewal. It is in knowing God that we choose to go on trusting God. The only alternative is not to trust, which is effectively to deny our faith.

> Either we view our lives in terms of our belief in God, and the conclusions which we are entitled to draw from that; or our outlook is based upon a rejection of God and the corresponding denials. We may either "withdraw" ourselves from the way of faith in God [Heb 10:38], or else we may live by faith in God. The very terms suggest corresponding ways of life. As a man believes so is he. A man's belief determines his conduct. The just, the righteous, shall live by faith; or, in other words, the man who lives by faith is righteous. On the other hand the man who "draws back" is unrighteous because he is not living by faith. Here is the great watershed of life, and all of us are on one side of it or the other. . . . Either my life is based on faith or it is not. If it is not, it does not much matter what my views may be, or whether I am controlled by political, social, economic, or any other considerations. What matters is whether I am accepting God's rule or not.[2]

---

[2]D. Martin Lloyd-Jones, *From Fear to Faith* (Leicester, U.K.: Inter-Varsity Press, 1953), p. 50.

Islamic rhetoric refers to Christians as "infidels"—i.e., unbelievers. Perhaps that is more true than we might like to admit. Where is our trust placed when life gets tough and the world (or our world) falls to pieces?

Because we know God will act in judgment, we will live by prayer. Habakkuk had received some shattering news. His own people were about to fall under the sword of Babylon, though the hand that wielded that sword would be none other than Yahweh their God. Yes, Babylon too would eventually face the wrath of God for their arrogant, destructive, oppressive greed. That was the theme of the bulk of Habakkuk 2. So the future looked bleak indeed. The judgment of God would fall on Israel and their enemies alike. What is the response of those who know God?

For Habakkuk it was to turn to prayer. It is a remarkable feature of the book that Habakkuk 1 is a conversation in prayer between Habakkuk and God—setting out Habakkuk's problems. Then Habakkuk 2 is a declaration of God's coming judgment. This is then followed immediately in Habakkuk 3 by another lengthy prayer, which comes to a remarkable and triumphant conclusion.

It begins in a remarkable way too, as we see in Habakkuk 3:2.

> LORD, I have heard of your fame;
>> I stand in awe of your deeds, O LORD.
> Renew them in our day,
>> in our time make them known;
>> in wrath remember mercy. (Hab 3:2)

Like so many of the great prayers of the Old Testament (as we saw in chapter five), this one makes three key moves. Habakkuk recalls God's great acts in the past, with appropriate awe; he then asks God to do again what he had so marvelously done before; and he asks God to remember mercy even in the midst of deserved judgment.

This is the prayer of one who knows God. He knows the awesome history of God; he knows the contemporary power of God; and he knows the merciful character of God. And he brings all that knowledge of God to bear on the problem he is facing.

For us, likewise, to recognize that events in our world today may involve elements of God's judgment does not paralyze prayer. We do not just say, "If that's how God is going to act, then there is no point in us praying." On the contrary, such knowledge motivates and energizes prayer. ·

That's what we see in other similar cases in the Bible. Think of Abraham, again, praying for Sodom in the wake of God's declared judgment. Think of Jeremiah, praying for the people of Judah, until God told him to stop because they were past praying for (Jer 14:11). Think of Jeremiah telling the exiles to pray even for Babylon (Jer 29:7)! Think of Daniel praying three times a day, in the midst of his career in the government service of Nebuchadnezzar (Dan 6).

Our enemies may indeed stand under the judgment of God. All the more reason to pray for them, according to Jesus (Mt 5:44). Judgment lies in the hand of God. Prayer is the weapon of love that he puts into our hands.

Because God will defend his people, we will live without fear (Ps 46:2; Hab 3:16-19).

> God is our refuge and strength,
>> an ever-present help in trouble.
> *Therefore we will not fear.* (Ps 46:1-2, italics added)

This is not sheer bravado. Nor is it a complete absence of natural physical fear in the face of suffering and death. Habakkuk was clearly very frightened indeed and he doesn't deny the physiological dimensions of it.

I heard and my heart pounded,
  my lips quivered at the sound;
decay crept into my bones,
  and my legs trembled. (Hab 3:16)

Paul urged Christians not to "grieve like the rest of men, who have no hope" (1 Thess 4:13). He did not mean that Christians should not experience the normal grief of bereavement—but that their grief should be transformed by hope. So should fear. The common biblical command, "Do not be afraid" (it is said to be the statistically most repeated command in the Bible), does not mean that believers should never experience the normal feelings of being afraid in dangerous circumstances. But it certainly does mean that natural fear is transformed by faith in the living God and his eternal protection.

Nor is this refusal to give way to fear merely a failure to face up to the real facts of the situation and all its dangers. Habakkuk knew exactly what enemy invasion would mean: the systematic destruction of the country's agricultural supplies and all the horror of siege, starvation and death. But even as he faces such a prospect, he refuses to give up his trust in God. The concluding words of his book are deservedly famous, for their resolute trust in God even in the face of impending calamity. Here is a man who knows his God.

Yet I will wait patiently for the day of calamity
  to come on the nation invading us.
Though the fig tree does not bud
  and there are no grapes on the vines,
though the olive crop fails

and the fields produce no food,
though there are no sheep in the pen
and no cattle in the stalls,
yet I will rejoice in the LORD,
I will be joyful in God my Savior. (Hab 3:16-18)

***Because God will be* exalted, *we will live for God's* mission.** The final verse of Habakkuk (apart from his instruction to the orchestra!), is surprisingly upbeat. In the wake of the section just quoted, you might have expected something along the lines of keeping one's head down until the storm has passed. If the world is in such a mess, and God's judgment is on the way, best keep a low profile, stay out of harm's way, and hold onto your faith. Not Habakkuk. God had given him a revelation that was to be read while running like a messenger (Hab 2:2). So Habakkuk would run, and not just on the flat. With God's strength, he would stride over the mountains.

The Sovereign LORD is my strength;
he makes my feet like the feet of a deer,
he enables me to go on the heights. (Hab 3:19)

So the closing picture of Habakkuk is of joy, strength, speed and climbing, not sitting back or opting out. Here is a man who knows God, and knows where his strength comes from. And he knows that he has a message from God to deliver.

We live in dangerous times, but God's mission goes on, as it has done through all the dangerous times and darkest eras of history. The first Christian century that gave birth to the New Testament was no picnic for the messengers of the gospel. That didn't stop them. They responded to the mission of God as it was entrusted to them by Jesus and took the dangers in their stride. After all, Jesus did not say, "Go and make disciples of all the *safe* nations."

Christian mission has never depended on favorable circumstances, peace and tranquility. We pray for such circumstances, of course, as Paul told us to, since they do facilitate the spread of the gospel and growth of the church (1 Tim 2:1-4). But we are not dependent on them.

What motivates and drives our mission is *God's* ultimate goal to be known and exalted in all the earth. That is the focus of God's reign, the purpose of God's sovereignty within history. If we claim to know this God, then we had better be found obedient to his call to share his mission, and face even the extreme challenges of our dangerous world in his strength and with his protection.

CONCLUSION

Faith, prayer, courage, mission. All are active, dynamic words. Once again we see how far removed "knowing God" is from mere pietism or the cultivation of some mystical dimension of our inner selves. Habakkuk and the author of Psalm 46 doubtless did have a close personal knowledge of their God. But what they affirm here is no subjective emotion. They build their confidence on strong affirmations about God's rule in nature and history, over creation and over the nations. It cannot have been any easier to do that in their day than in ours (just because they are "in the Bible"). Rather, their tough commitment and confidence against all visible odds, stem from a radical understanding of who this living God, the LORD God of Hosts, truly is, and what it means to say that he is "with us."

Epilogue

How Do You Know That You Know God?

Some of the chapters on our journey of biblical discovery have focused on the more personal ways in which some biblical characters knew God, like Abraham and Moses. Others have reflected on the personal implications for faith and worship that we find when the psalmists talk about knowing God. But much of our journey has explored what it meant for the people of God as a whole to know their God, or for other peoples to come to know Israel's God. In the process we have discovered enormous truths about God, about his character and action, and of course about his nature as our heavenly Father. But you may still be left wondering, "Do I really know this God? How can I *know* that I know him?"

Someone spoke to me during the conference that I mentioned in the preface, after I had given several Bible addresses on the theme of knowing God. "I want to know God," he said, "but I don't seem to, or at least I can't claim to." This was a mature Christian—not someone on the edge of faith and conversion. It sounded like he was unsure what the experience of knowing God was supposed to be like, and longed for some clarity or reassurance. This is not surprising, since people's subjective and personal experience of God varies a lot. It varies according to what we've been taught. It varies according to what we therefore come to expect. It varies according to the latest testimony we may have heard. And it certainly seems to vary according to different personality and temperament types.

There are some who are very ready with expressions like, "God just spoke to me"; "I just know God wants me to do this, or that"; "I really felt God's presence in the room." It's hard to doubt their sincerity, though one sometimes might request further clarification of exactly what such claims actually mean. I have no doubt that some people do indeed have a direct and physiological consciousness of God, especially when they pray. One of my friends, when we would be praying together, would physically tremble as she "felt God" (as she put it), and I know her to be a godly and sensible woman, spiritually mature and seasoned in Christian ministry. And in view of the biblical precedents for the impact of God's presence, it would be foolish to deny such elemental ways of "knowing God" quite directly. Indeed, I sometimes envied the simplicity and directness of my friend's testimony to her awareness of God's presence.

On the other hand, there are many people, including myself most of the time, for whom knowing God is much more matter-of-fact and down-to-earth. We don't hear voices or feel shivers. We don't get transported, or "slain," or ecstatic. We don't "feel the wind of the Spirit," or any of the other common expressions in certain Christian groups and cultures. And yet we are constantly aware of the reality of God. God is simply "there" as the whole foundation, background, foreground and ambience of our daily lives. Knowing God is simply a dimension of living. We slightly modify the words of a popular song:

> Father God I wonder how *I'd manage* to exist
> Without the knowledge of your parenthood
> And your loving care . . .

I sometimes think it is a bit like marriage. "Knowing your spouse," in a happy and positive married relationship, does not always mean being physically close together, always talking or touching, always having intense feelings of being "in love" (however wonderful, essential and assuring such times are). And yet, being married and knowing him or her is part of the bedrock of daily existence. It is a condition of life, consciously or subconsciously, not something you have to "feel" or "experience" every moment in order to know its reality. Maybe we could learn more from the depths of our human relationships about what it means to be in a "knowing" relationship with God.

And yet, and yet . . . however much our doctrinal heads tell us that we do know God, our hearts still long for the assurance to go along with the faith. We want to be sure. We want to *know* that we know God. Can we have that assurance?

Absolutely yes, says John!

Now by this we may be sure that we know him, if we obey his commandments. Whoever says, "I have come to know him," but does not obey his commandments, is a liar, and in such a person the truth does not exist; but whoever obeys his word, truly in this person the love of God has reached perfection. By this we may be sure that we are in him: whoever says, "I abide in him," ought to walk just as he walked. (1 Jn 2:3-6 NRSV)

The test and the proof are practical. One of the passionate concerns that the first letter of John addresses is precisely that of assurance. John longs for his readers not only to have the right doctrine (to believe the truth), and not only to have the right ethics (to live in the right way), but also to have full assurance of their standing in relation to God and to other children of God within the fellowship of other believers. So he wants us not only to know God, but to know that we know him.

First John 2:3 is actually a quite remarkable epistemological claim. Epistemology is concerned not only with knowledge in itself, but with *how* we come to know what we know, and *by what criteria* we can evaluate various claims to know anything. So here, John does not simply say, "This is how we know him, by obeying him." That in itself would be true, of course. We have seen that most clearly in chapter six above, in the words of Jeremiah 22:15-16: to do righteousness and justice—that is to know God. But John goes further than that. Not only do we know God through obeying him, but also we know that we know God through obeying him. Our obedience is the means of assurance as well as the source of the knowledge itself. Or to put it in more technical language, the epistemological foundation for our knowledge of God lies in the practical realm of obeying him.

And for our encouragement, this is how it was for Jesus also. There is no question, of course, but that Jesus knew God. We began this book observing the astonishing intimacy of his daily communion with his Father in prayer. But even for him, this knowledge of God was both expressed and assured in obedience, in doing his Father's will (as he so often put it). Indeed, as Hebrews observed, part of the very purpose of his incarnate life as a real human being was that he learned through the experience of earthly suffering what obedience means for humans like us (Heb 5:8). There was a dimension of knowing God as Father that, even for Jesus God's Son, could only come through obedience and the suffering it involved.

So then, returning to 1 John, if you want to be sure that you know God, then walk as Jesus walked, live as Jesus lived (1 Jn 2:6)—in obedience to your heavenly Father. Then, *by that and in that,* you will know that you know him.

The friendship of the LORD is for those who fear him,
and he makes his covenant known to them. (Ps 25:14, NRSV)

You are my friends if you do what I command you. I do not call
you servants any longer, because the servant does not know
what the master is doing; but I have called you friends, because
I have made known to you everything that I have heard from
my Father. (Jn 15:14-15 NRSV)

The psalmist and Jesus together make the point very clear: intimacy with God flows from reverence and obedience toward him. As he makes himself known to us, we assuredly come to know him.

So let us not be discouraged by stories of people who speak of mysterious experiences of knowing God, or the testimonies of those who sound so much more spiritual than ourselves. We can only look on the outside of such claims; the Lord looks on the inside and sees the heart. What does he see in your own? If he sees a heart that is set on obeying him in daily practical life—faithfully, humbly, with patience, perseverance, courage and joy—then he says, "I know you, and you know me!" For

if anyone obeys his word, God's love is truly made complete in him. This is how we know we are in him. (1 Jn 2:5)

Scripture Index

Knowing Jesus Through the Old Testament

We cannot know Jesus without knowing his story. But the debate over who he is rages on. Has the Bible bound Christians to a narrow and mistaken notion of Jesus? Should we listen to other Gospels, other sayings of Jesus, that enlarge and correct a mistaken story? To answer these questions we need to know what story Jesus claimed for himself. Christopher Wright is convinced that Jesus' own story is rooted in the story of Israel. In *Knowing Jesus Through the Old Testament* he traces the life of Christ as it is illuminated by the Old Testament. And he describes God's design for Israel as it is fulfilled in the story of Jesus.

Knowing the Holy Spirit Through the Old Testament

We tend to think of the Holy Spirit as the straggler of the Trinity, a latecomer in God's interaction with the world. But our first introduction to the Holy Spirit is not the drama of Pentecost in the second chapter of Acts. We first meet the Holy Spirit in the second verse of the Bible, hovering there, speaking the world into existence. Christopher Wright begins here and traces the Holy Spirit through the pages of the Old Testament. We see the Third Person of the Trinity in the decrees of prophets and psalmists, in the actions of judges and craftspeople, in the anointing of kings and the promise of a new creation. Knowable and discernable in the Old Testament, the Holy Spirit is thus eminently knowable to us.